Voices Unheard:
Indigenous and Tribal Literatures

Voices Unheard
Indigenous and Tribal Literatures

A Festschrift in Honour of Professor B. Yadava Raju

Edited by

A. Karunaker
B. Vijaya
Nageshwar Rao Konda

Prestige Books International
New Delhi

Published by
Prestige Books International
New Delhi 110 060
prestigebooks@gmail.com
Phone: 9818755529

Associate Office
11B, Broomwood Road
London SW11 6HU

Associate Office
P.O. Box 2250
Sydney 2001

ISBN: 978-81-943009-5-3

Printed in India

Contents

Poems

Professor B. Yadava Raju
A Tribute

Born in a family of modest background at Devnoor village of Warangal district, Dr Biruduraj Yadava Raju is the second son of late Sri Biruduraj Veera Narasimha Raju and Smt. Kamala Devi. Dr. Raju achieved success the hard way, by sheer perseverance and hard work. He did his Masters in English Literature with First Division from Kakatiya University in 1981. Later, he obtained PGDTE from CIEFL in 1987; M.Phil. degree from Kakatiya University on the Short Stories of Bernard Malamud in 1991; Ph.D. degree from Osmania University on the Fiction of V.S. Naipaul, under the supervision of Dr. Kuppa Srinivasa Sastry, in 1995. Dr. Raju started his career as an ad hoc lecturer at Kothagudem School of Mines, Osmania University, Kothagudem, in September 1982. He got a regular appointment at the same place in 1985. He was transferred to the University P.G. College, Secunderabad in October 1988, and served the University for thirty-six long years. He has held several academic positions in the department and in the University in his long years of service. He served the department as Chairman, Board of Studies, and Head of the Department, and later as Dean, Faculty of Arts, Osmania University. After a successful tenure as Dean for two years, he was appointed Member Secretary, Telangana State Eligibility Test in 2018, and conducted successfully the State Eligibility Test (paper-based) in 2018 and (computer-based) in 2019. Besides an academic administrator, Dr. Raju has been a sincere and serious researcher also. He published more than 20 research articles and edited 12 text books for the Undergraduate degree courses in Telangana and Andhra Pradesh States. Apart from these publications, he has been actively participating in the National and International seminars conducted from time to time. He presented more than 20 papers in different Seminars and Conferences. He was the Convener for the 62nd All India English Teachers' Conference in 2018 and Advisor for the International Conference on "Voices Unheard: Indigenous and Tribal Literature in English and English Translation" in 2019. He was also instrumental in reviving the *Osmania Journal of English Studies*, published by the Department of English, Osmania University. He designed along Add-on course along with his colleagues which was prescribed for the Postgraduate students at the University level in 2010-2011.

A multi-faceted personality, we find in him vibrancy, dynamism and tenacity to explore new areas of study and research. His expertise attracted many students, scholars and young teachers to develop unique arguments in the areas of Postcolonial Literature, New Literatures, Translation and Bhasha Literatures, in addition to the Canonical Literature. He has guided six Ph.D. scholars including one research scholar from Iran. Presently, eight research scholars are working under his supervision.

We find in Professor Yadava Raju a committed teacher-administrator, a sagacious scholar who has the courage of conviction as a critic. While pragmatic in approach, he has a vision and can lead the way by setting an example. An unassuming person, he has uncanny ability of winning hearts of people. No wonder, he commands immense respect as a versatile scholar and a humane person—full of milk of human kindness, as Shakespeare would say. A genial person, true scholar and able administrator—Professor Yadava Raju has all the qualities of head and heart. Thanks, Professor Yadava Raju, for your positive spirit and for inspiring us all these years. We wish you all the best in your future endeavours.

Preface

A. KARUNAKER
B. VIJAYA
NAGESHWAR RAO KONDA

Stories are an integral part of who we are as peoples. For aborigines and adivasis, traditional storytelling was mostly based on the spoken word. For generations, children learned about their culture and their history through stories their elders told them. People of all ages gathered around a storyteller to hear ancient tales that served as important lessons. This laid the foundation for the oral narratives. Oral narratives provided space to the unheard voices.

Tribal and indigenous literatures form a rich repertoire in the oral tradition which now is being written, translated and anthologized. Replete with tropes and metaphors, most of them from mythical traditions, it not only traces narratives of cultural traditions and conventions but also subverts and explodes social hierarchies, structures and forms and questions societal mores and norms.

The anthology, *Voices Unheard: Indigenous and Tribal Literatures*, consists of twelve papers. The first paper "Tribal Wisdom in Proverbs" written by Paritosh Chandra Dugar examines various proverbs that are capable of performing different functions depending on the text and the context in which they are used. Some that imparts information, few that satirize social hills and few that ridicule the situation. The entire paper throws light on the tribal wisdom in the form of proverbs through different cultural, linguistic, anthropological, epistemological, ethical, metaphysical, literary, religious and so on.

Shruti Das in her paper "Precarity of Existence: Indigenous People in the Andaman Islands, a Reading of Pankaj Sekhsaria's *The Last Wave*" observes the crisis of existence and survival faced by the indigenous people who lack agency and are on the fringes of the society. The paper explores the subjectivity and lack of agency that chronicles the life and livelihood of the tribes of the Andaman and Nicobar Islands.

Jagriti Upadhyaya's paper "A Feminist Reading of Select Indigenous Narratives from Rajasthan" discusses the rich literary tradition of the indigenous tribes like Bhils, the Kalbelias, the Langas, the Manganiyas, and the Mers of Rajasthan. It also traces the narratives of cultural traditions and conventions of the Indigenous tribes of Rajasthan.

Anita Gua Hembrom's paper "Relevance of Santhali Literature in Present-Day Translations" explores the inclusion and exclusion policies adopted by the translators of the Santhali literature. It voices the deliberate exclusion of the Santhali texts as a matter of representational politics of discourses.

The paper "Oral Narratives: Cultural Deterioration of the Banjara Tribe in India" by B. Vijaya is an attempt to demonstrate the cultural deterioration of the Banjara Tribe in India. The focus of the paper is to sensitize the change in the cultural practices, especially the present marriage system that deteriorates from 'bride price' to 'dowry system,' an import in the Banjara Culture from the caste stratified Hindu society that causes many dowry deaths. The paper also documents the original six-month wedding ceremony of the Banjara Tribe in India, especially in Telangana and Andhra Pradesh. It also narrates the oral songs involved in the process of Marriage in which, there is no role of the middleman or the priest.

Anju P.S. in the paper "'We are not Showpieces': The Unheard Voices of Kani Tribes of Agasthyarkoodam" traces the consequences and issues involved in the conversion of tribal settlements into tourist spots through a special study on Agasthyarkoodam hill, the second highest peak in Kerala, situated on the Southern-most part of Western Ghats. Kanikkar, also known as Kanis are one among largest tribal population in Kerala, who are found in and around the Agasthyarkoodam Hills. Their settlement, rituals, life, culture, and customs are highly embedded in the Agasthyarkoodam hill ranges.

"Mapping the Touchstones of Indigenous, Tribal and Subaltern Literatures in English" by Nageshwar Rao Konda argues about the marginalized voices and how they were deliberately excluded from the mainstream literature. He also tries to touch up on the various concerns, theories related to the Indigenous Literature in the multi-lingual context.

"Tracing the Untouchables: A Study of Socio-Cultural Life of Dusadhs" by Ritu Chourasiya examines the rich folk literature of the Dusadh community in the state of Bihar. The paper also argues against the misrepresentation of Dusadh community as mere looters, highway robbers, arrogant, uncivilized in the dominant narratives and that in Dusadh community's perspectives robbery, looting were act of heroism for the welfare of their community and also a form of protest against atrocities faced by them in the society.

P. Shobha in her paper "Native American Struggle: A Study of James Welch's *Winter in the Blood* and Sherman Alexie's *Reservation Blues*" discusses the native American struggle and the idea of cultural displacement in James Welch's *Winter in the Blood* and Sherman Alexie's *Reservation Blues* focuses on the despair, poverty, violence and alcoholism both on and off the reservation.

"Exposition on Canadian Feminism: A Comparative Study of Margaret Atwood's *The Edible Woman* and Margaret Laurence's *The Diviners*" by V. Jyothi presents the evolving status of women in Canada.

The paper "The Insights of Sexuality in Disabled Women" by Bolla Madhavi presents the problems of the disabled women in terms of objectification of their bodies containing the usual desires of sexuality, love and acceptance of the disabled body.

"Sabarimala Untold: The Brahminisation of an Adivasi Deity" by Jobinraj R.V & Dhinil Sen attempts to portray the struggle for the revival of Arayar community. The concepts of 'double jeopardy,' namely caste and gender, are scrutinized. The Mala Arayars today are different from their historical counterparts of 19th century, both in thoughts and actions. The current socio-political climate has only made them stronger to fight for their rights.

Tribal Wisdom in Proverbs

PARITOSH CHANDRA DUGAR

What is a proverb? The question might have multiple answers, yet perhaps not one of them might qualify to be treated as a universal definition. Other than all scholarly definition attempts by paremiologists across the world, Wolfgang Mieder once sought, as he mentions in his essay "Popular Views of the Proverb", to elicit spontaneous responses to the simple question "How do you define a proverb?" from students, colleagues, and friends. In answer, he could gather a sample of 55 definitions. He then performed a word analysis of the definitions by counting the frequency of nouns occurring in them. His list of nouns with their frequency indicated in parentheses is as follows: "wisdom (20); phrase (14); sentence, saying (13); statement (12); folk (10); situation (9); expression (7); life (6); truth, moral, people (5); generation, experience, advice, lesson, word (4); principle, analogy, belief, behavior, meaning, action (3); language, generalization, attitude, message, opinion, picture, comment, thought, comparison, tradition, rule, viewpoint (2); origin, idea, occurrence, philosophy, knowledge, conclusion, prejudice, folklore, paradigm, threat, form, norm, nature, value, ideal, image, poetry, author, admonition, rhyme, alliteration, witticism, brevity, profundity, clarity, precision, culture, condition, concern (1)."

Mieder's task eventually led him to arrive at a composite definition of a proverb. He says, "From this [word analysis] it becomes clear that a proverb is commonly thought of as 'a phrase, saying, sentence, statement or expression of the folk which contains above all wisdom, truth, morals, experience, lessons and advice concerning life and which has been handed down from generation to generation.'" And the shortest general definition of a proverb he derived from the composite one was: "A proverb is wisdom expressed in a sentence." Mieder's intention behind the task was actually to study how the common people, not the scholar, look at a proverb. However, most scholars in their attempts to come to terms with a universal definition of a proverb came up with useful generalizations about the characteristics of a proverb, the indicators or markers of proverbiality, the nature, functions, and classifications of proverbs.

To begin with, let us consider Shirley L. Arora's observation in her essay "The Perception of Proverbiality": "Probably the most consistently accepted generalization concerning, in virtually any language, is that they [proverbs] are 'traditional,' and that is their traditionality—the sense of historically derived authority or of community-sanctioned wisdom that they convey—that makes them 'work.'" Arora considers metaphor as one of the most effective indicators of proverbiality. In her essay she refers to Silverman Weinreich, a folklorist, to emphasize the semantic markers of proverbiality. She says, "Other semantic markers mentioned by Silverman Reinreich include semantic parallelism, paradox, irony, and sharp contrasts and surprising comparisons." No doubt, rhyme stands as an important phonic marker of proverbiality. Apart from being traditional, a proverb must characteristically be a grammatically self-contained expression, a complete sentence and a full statement in order to be differentiated from other similar language items.

Trench, a proverb theorist, suggested three major characteristics of a proverb: "Shortness, Sense, and Salt." By 'shortness' he meant that a proverb "must be succinct, utterable in a breath" (qtd. Dabaghi et al 808). The 'sense' for him is "sometimes scarified to alliteration" (Dabaghi et al 808). And about the 'salt' he asserts that "a proverb must have salt, that is, besides its good sense it must in its manner and outward form being pointed and pungent, having a sting in it, a barb which shall not suffer it to drop lightly from the memory" (qtd. in Dabaghi et al 808).

Proverbs are capable of performing different roles or functions as speech acts depending on the text and the context in which they are used. Some proverbs are meant to impart information and can be analyzed on the locutionary speech level, while some others are used to convey metaphorical meaning and thus need to be interpreted on the illocutionary speech level. Yet a few other proverbs may be judged as perlocutionary speech acts, especially when they generate noticeable results related to the listeners' feelings, thoughts or actions.

No doubt, proverbs make the language a more vivid and powerful tool of communication. A response gains more weight when we speak using a general opinion as embodied by a proverb. In his book *Proverbs Are Never out of Season: Popular Wisdom in the Modern Age*, Mieder argues, "By employing proverbs in our speech we wish to strengthen our arguments, express generalizations, influence or manipulate other people, rationalize our own shortcomings, question certain behavioral patterns, satirize social ills, poke fun at ridiculous situations." According to Archer Taylor, "As a guide to life's problems, the proverb summarizes a situation, passes a judgment or offers a course of action" (Study of Proverbs). In Mieder's opinion, traditional proverbs are still relevant in modern times and employed "to moralize, to instruct, to advise, and to reflect on everyday occurrences" (*Proverbs* 58). It means proverbs are still being used for a didactic purpose. In personal interactions, proverbs are used "to warn of danger, tell people how to behave and how to not behave, advise or give direct orders and prohibitions." Proverbs can also be "a tool by means of which we can discredit or mock someone or criticize someone or a situation" (Krasuska, Proverbs and their functions) in a polite or indirect manner.

In view of the fact that proverbs are carriers of the community's wisdom, they can be analyzed from different cultural perspectives: linguistic anthropological, epistemological, ethical, metaphysical, literary, religious and so on.

A linguistic anthropological examination of proverbs can tell us about the relationship between culture and language, how language can affect the attitudes and behaviour of the people. For example, Robert Frost in his poem "Mending Wall" refers to his neighbour who blindly believes in his father's saying (proverb) "Good fences make good neighbors." The force of the proverb lying in its metaphorical and alliterative language as well as its traditionality influences the simple-minded neighbour and makes him absolutely impervious to the poet's logic "Something there is that doesn't love a wall."

A metaphysical study of proverbs can offer insights into people's attitude to life, God, and the world. An epistemological analysis of proverbs may enable us to understand how the people of a given community thought of knowledge and knowledge production. An ethical interpretation of proverbs might enlighten us about how the people behave, how they view vice and virtue, good and bad.

On the basis of the above perspectives proverbs can be categorized into different types such as anthropological proverbs, metaphysical proverbs, epistemological proverbs, ethical proverbs. However, scholars have attempted to classify proverbs taking into account other features or characteristics of proverbs. For example, Dabaghi refers to Norrick's categorization of proverbs according to the type of figuration they use: synecdoche proverbs, metaphoric proverbs, metonymic proverbs, hyperbolic proverbs, paradoxical proverbs (Dabaghi 808-9).

In synecdoche proverbs, the literal meaning is quite different from the figurative meaning. For example, 'Fair words break no bones.' In metaphoric proverbs, the named object symbolizes some characteristic attribute: 'Fair play is a jewel.' Metonymic proverbs are founded on association between a thing named in literal terms and the thing intended." One example of this type is: 'One who has a fair wife needs more than two eyes.' Here the 'eye' stands for the 'sight.' Hyperbolic proverbs are based on exaggeration. For example, in the proverb 'Faint heart never won fair lady' the word 'never' makes the statement hyperbolic (exaggerated). In paradoxical proverbs, there is a logical contradiction entailing the possibility of a second interpretation. One example of this type is: 'Fair is not fair, but that which pleases,' and the other is: 'A man's house is heaven and hell as well.'

Regardless of the type, almost all proverbs are founded on communal experiences and observations which are usually consistent with the worldview of the people of the community. Proverbs are therefore capable of providing insights into "activities, interests, and philosophy of the people who created them" (Todd et al 385) and who use them. In the words of Francis Bacon, "The genius, wit and spirit of a nation are discovered in its proverbs." The importance of proverbs as a means of exploring and understanding a community's culture, life, philosophy, religion, values cannot be denied. It is generally admitted that nothing defines a culture as distinctly as its language, and the element of language that best encapsulates a society's values and beliefs is its proverbs. Since proverbs as a folklore genre belong to oral tradition and are generationally-transferred carriers of folk wisdom, they can be used to get glimpses of the culture and philosophy of a community, especially a tribal community which is primarily characterized by orality rather than written communication.

The present paper analyses some common proverbs of the Bhil tribe of India from linguistic anthropological, metaphysical, epistemological, and ethical perspectives in order understand the community's culture and wisdom; its people's attitudes to life and the world.

In the tribal heritage of India, the Bhils have had a significant contribution. Bhil, the biggest tribe of Western India and one of the biggest of the country is known for its rich treasure of culture. The Bhils are recognized as the oldest living inhabitants of southern Rajasthan and adjoining parts of states like Gujarat, Madhya Pradesh, and Maharashtra belonging to the Dravidian ethnic type. In Rajasthan, the Bhils are concentrated in Dungarpur, Banswara, Udaipur, and Chittorgarh districts. The Bhil is sometimes called 'Vanputra' (child of the forest) or 'Pal Indra' (Lord of the pass).

The Bhils' language, believed once to have been distinct, is now not so different from the languages spoken by their non-tribal neighbours. The dialects spoken by the Bhils are known as Bhili and Vagdi. Bhili shows Mewari influence, while Vagdi is closer to Gujarati.

The name Bhil is believed to have been derived from the Dravidian word for a bow, which is a typical weapon of the tribe.

Most of the Bhil proverbs are ethical in nature. Many of them seem to focus on business ethics, human conduct, importance of loyalty and integrity in human relationships, personal ethics, and social ethics. Some of the Bhil proverbs illustrating these ethical dimensions are as follows:

1. *Zewun kam, tewun dam.* (*Zewun* = as is/ are; *kam* = labour/ work; *tewun* = so be; *dam* = wages). This proverb prescribes payment of wages to workers according to their labour. The principle is practically good for the progress of all kinds of business. The proverb seems to be based on the common observation that if wages are not paid according to the quantity and quality of the work done, it affects the workers' efficiency adversely. Underpaid workers feel demoralized and demotivated while overpaid ones grow arrogant and complacent.
2. *Zewun dam, tewun kam.* (*zewun* = as is/ are; *dam* = wages; *tewun* = so be; *kam* = labour/ work). This proverb reveals the

expectation of workers in business. It underlines the workers' awareness of their right to just wages. Interestingly enough, the same proverb may be exploited by shirkers to rationalize their indolence and inefficiency by blaming their wages for their lower outputs.

3. *Danto ni rih hothon par nin kaadwi*. (*Danto* = teeth; *ni* = of; *rih* = anger; *hothon* = lips; *par* = on; *nin* = not/ don't; *kaadwi* = express). In a metaphorical way, this proverb asks us not to let our anger affect our language. The teeth's anger should not travel to our lips. The proverb emphasizes patience and restraint as part of wise human conduct.
4. *Khai peene ghar na danda gane*. (*Khai* = after eating; *peene* = after drinking; ghar = house; *na* = of; *danda* = rafters; *gane* = count). Having had drinks and meal in the host's house, he counts the rafters of the house. Being ungrateful and treacherous, he secretly transfers the crucial information about the house to the host's enemy. In fact, this proverb metaphorically condemns ingratitude and treachery and cautions us against perfidious people.
5. *Roko, bhai, thok! Udar, bhai thob*. (*Roko* = if cash; *bhai* = brother/ customer; *thok* = take; *udar* = if credit; *thob* = wait). This is yet another proverb which sets a principle for the growth of a business. It says: 'If cash, brother, take! If credit, brother wait!' We are familiar with this piece of practical wisdom. The pithy and succinct way in which it is conveyed catches one's attention.

Some of the Bhil proverbs are reflections on human nature and serve as guide to good conduct. For example: 1. *Aam pakya neeche lulle, erand uncho jaay*. (*Aam* = mango; *pakya* = when ripened; *neeche* = downward; *lulle* = hang; *erand* = Ricinus communis, a type of medicinal plant; *uncho* = upward; *jaay* = go/ move). This proverb figuratively draws a sharp distinction between a good man and a bad man. It says that a good man grows humbler when he becomes prosperous while a bad man becomes haughtier and greedier.

From an epistemological perspective the following proverbs seem worthy of consideration:

1. *Bhaniya pan ganiya ni*. (*Bhaniya* = studied; *pan* = but; *ganiya* = assimilated; *ni* = not). The proverb suggests that knowledge obtained from books remains imperfect and futile unless it is assimilated through experience/ experimentation. It means that authoritative knowledge of which books are a great source is epistemologically advantageous and relevant only when it is backed by empirical knowledge.
2. *Khet ke nipaj to baad hi bataa de*. (*Khet* = farm/ field; *ke* = of; *nipaj* = crop; *baad* = fencing; *hi* = itself; *bataa* = speak/ tell). By looking at the fencing one can have an estimation of the crop. Better the fencing, the more valuable the crop. The proverb clearly indicates how logic and observation can be a source of knowledge. The proverb presents a parameter by which the preciousness of a thing or the importance of a person can be judged. The more precious a thing is, the better it is protected. So is true for persons.

Certain Bhil proverbs are found to have metaphysical ingredients. For example:

1. *Karam ma likhya bhatta, te hun kare bhagwan*. (Karam = destiny/ fate; ma = in; likhya = written; bhatta = stones/ unproductive things; te = then; hun = what; kare = do; bhagwan = God). What can God do if you are already ill-fated. This proverb metaphysically reveals the Bhils' attitude to God, life, and destiny. The Bhils do not deny the presence of a benevolent God, but at the same time they do recognize the role of fate or destiny, which marks a deterministic conception of life.
2. *Ram rakhe ke dam*. (*Ram* = name of a Hindu deity; *rakhe* = save/ take care of; *ke* = or; *dam* = hot touch). The Bhils' metaphysical understanding that God isn't always merciful is

revealed through this proverb. According to them, sometimes God saves and sometimes the 'dam' (the traditional method of healing using a hot iron stick to burn the diseased part of the body) saves the ailing person.

Some Bhil proverbs can be analyzed in linguistic anthropological terms as they illustrate the influence of language on human behaviour. Such proverbs are culturally important in that they guide and determine interpersonal relationships as well as social behaviour. For example:

1. *Gher ne aangane me kutron ane bor ni palawno*. (*Gher* = house; *ne* = of; *aangane* = courtyard; *me* = in; *kutron* = dogs; *ane* = and; *bor* = Zizyphus mauritiana, a type of thorny tree; *ne* = not/ don't; *palawno* = rear/ grow). This proverb teaches the Bhil not to domesticate a dog nor to grow a 'bor' tree in his house. The dog is unpredictable and the 'bor' tree is harmful as it pricks. Figuratively, the proverb asks the Bhil to keep at bay any unpredictable or mischievous person.
2. *Ghee gaal khawaade in baat sab hamle*. (Ghee = butter; gaal = mixing; khawaade = offer as food; in = this; baat = speech; sab = all; hamle = follow). What people learn from this proverb is the fact that those who speak gently and softly receive attention from people. They can even become leaders. Politeness and sweetness command confidence.
3. *Bhang peebo soro lerna lebo doro*. (*Bhang* = Cannabis sativa, a type of plant whose leaves produce intoxicating effect; *peebo* = drink; *soro* = easy; *lerna* = results; *lebo* = bear; *doro* = difficult). Here 'bhang' stands for any kind of intoxicating substance. Figuratively, drinking bhang means doing any kind of mischievous or criminal activity. The proverb warns that it is easy to drink bhang (it is easy to commit a crime), but it is difficult to bear the consequences. This cautionary advice seems to be intended to prevent people from treading the path of crime and sin.

It can be seen from the foregoing analysis of Bhil proverbs that proverbs are embodiments of tribal wisdom as they carry ethical, linguistic anthropological, epistemological, and metaphysical ingredients which constitute the philosophy and the world view of the Bhil tribe. The present study, which is by no means a comprehensive one, is a modest attempt to suggest the direction and potential for further research in the area of tribal proverbs.

Note: Most proverbs (translated from Bhili/ Vagdi) referred to in the text have been taken from: Leonhard Jungblut, "Bhil Wisdom in Proverbs and Phrases," *Primitive Man*. 18.3-4: 56-62. www.jstor.org/ stable; and Aparna Pareek and P.C. Trivedi, "Common Folk Proverbs in Relation to Environment and Plants in Rajasthan, India." *The Journal of the Indian Botanical Society*. 93.1-2 (2014): 100-4.

Works Cited

Arora, Shirley L. "The Perception of Proverbiality." *Proverb Studies*. 1.1 (1995): n.p. deproverbio.com/proverb-studies-journal/proverb-studies-issue-1

Dabaghi, Azizollah et al. "Proverbs from the Viewpoint of Translation." *Journal of Language Teaching and Research*. 1.6 (2010): 807-14.

Krasuska, Dorota. "Proverbs and their functions." www.profesor.pl/ mat/ n13/ n13_dkrasuska_020106_2php>

Mieder, Wolfgang. "Popular Views of the Proverb." *Proverb Studies*. 5.2 (1999): n.p. deproverbio.com/ proverb-studies-journal/ proverb-studies-issue-10

_____. *Proverbs Are Never Out of Season: Popular Wisdom in the Modern Age*. Oxford: Oxford UP, 1993.

Taylor, Archer. "The Study of Proverbs." *Proverb Studies*. 2.1 (1996): n.p. deproverbio.com/proverb-studies-journal/ proverb-studies-issue-3

Todd, Loreto and Hancock, Ian F. *International English Usage*. London: Croom Helm, 1986.

Precarity of Existence: Indigenous People in the Andaman Islands, A Reading of Pankaj Sekhsaria's *The Last Wave*

SHRUTI DAS

It is interesting to note that while we are almost paranoid in our concern regarding our own sustenance on earth, we summarily ignore the crisis of existence and survival faced by the indigenous people who lack agency and are in the fringes of society. Cultural anthropologists and sociologists have been trying to make us aware of the fact that the world is about to make extinct its original people, as economic and political theorists the world over have continued to ignore the anxiety in their feeble voices. Since time immemorial literature has been a chronicler and has been giving voice to this anxiety resulting from a nature-culture interface.

Pankaj Sekhsaria's depiction of the Andaman Islands in his novel, *The Last Wave: An Island Novel* (2014), is a prototype of the human-nature interface, whereby the pristine nature is corroded and indigenous people are corrupted. *The Last Wave* narrates the story of life of the people living in the Andaman Islands, a postcolony in the Bay of Bengal. Since there is no literature available by the Jarawa people, who unfortunately, do not even have a script of their own, I have chosen to analyze their subjectivity and lack of agency through the depiction of life in the Andamans in *The Last Wave* and through a dossier that chronicles the live and livelihood of the tribes of the Andaman and Nicobar Islands written by Pankaj Sekhsaria.

The Last Wave portrays the lives of the settlers from mainland India and the descendants from prisoners of the Andaman Jail, who have acquired land and colonize the Andaman Islands, its flora, fauna and the indigenous Jarawa people. Contemporary postcolonial studies interrogate such neocolonialisms and raises questions like: where to now in the wake of material development and expansion? This brings us to the pressing concern of subjectivity of nature and indigenous people and the corrosive forces of anthropogenic interventions. Subjectivity is determined by repression, victimization, a lack of opportunity to grow and this is what this paper intends to explore in the novel, *The Last Wave*. Making it part of the story of a group of researchers and their associates, Sekhsaria lays the narrative's ecological foundation. I propose to isolate specific features of subjectivity in order to address questions of ecological importance. To begin with, let us take for instance, these lines from *The Last Wave*: "There couldn't have been a greater irony—the Great Andamanese were on the verge of extinction [which] they did not know was coming. . . . 'God alone knows what else is going on – it could be a time bomb waiting to explode. The fuse perhaps has already been lit'" (127)

The lines cited above seem eerily prophetic. With the increase of capitalist material neo-colonialism, global warming and recent environmental disasters have become commonplace. Like the now extinct, Great Andamanese, even the most powerful of humans do not know what is coming their way. In the wake of this impending annihilation of one race after the other, an ecological consciousness has been growing amongst the human beings. Fear for their own future and a growing insecurity is plaguing them with existential questions like, have human beings permanently changed planet Earth? What are the chances of our survival in a planet constantly battered for the development of human civilization? And no one seems to have any convincing answers to these terrifying questions. Often enough contemporary literature fictionalizes reality and gives voice to this anxiety.

The textual world and the real world are inextricably connected, in that; the literary text reflects the natural world of its time through the author's depiction of the environment and human's relationship to it. The objective of this paper is to analyze *The Last Wave* with tools of postcolonial ecocriticism and show how this narrative tries to map the extent of exploitation, damage and change human beings have wrought on this earth which they have perpetually 'othered.' The expansion of the domain of postcolonial studies facilitates the analysis of culture and ideology in this novel using postcolonial ecocriticism as a framework. It claims to study the colonial history and political practice in the Andaman Islands. According to Vivek Chibber, at the outset the impulse of postcolonialism as a movement was "naturally directed toward the structures of colonial and neo-colonial domination." (2) Chibber cites John McLeod's argument regarding postcolonial theory as a theory relevant to anyone "joined by the common political and ethical commitment to challenging and questioning the practices and consequences of domination and subordination." (2) *The Last Wave* radically critiques and challenges subjectivity while questioning the practice and outcome of exploitation and domination of the Andaman Islands, its original inhabitants and its rainforests.

Pankaj Sekhsaria, the author of *The Last Wave: An Island Novel,* is a researcher, writer and environmentalist who has worked extensively in the field of environment and wildlife conservation with particular focus on the Andaman and Nicobar Islands. The depiction of the Andaman Islands in this novel gives a postcolonial construction of the environment of the Islands. In twenty four chapters a Prologue and an Epilogue, the novel portrays the lives and attitude of the settlers who have come from mainland India; the descendants from prisoners of the Andaman Jail, who have acquired aboriginal land on freedom from captivity; and the Jarawas, the original inhabitants of the Andaman Islands. The settlers' interface with the tropical rainforest and the indigenous Jarawa people of the islands is indeed a matter of concern for the writer. The novel set in the Andamans of pre-Tsunami times, in November 2003 (12) to 26 December 2004 (260), narrates the histories of the "local borns", the people who were born in the islands after their parents were released from the Andaman jails; the labour force brought by the British from mainland India and the people deported to these Islands along with the histories of the encounter and interface of these people with the Jarawa, the aboriginal inhabitants of the Islands and the rainforest.

History of a land and its people forms an integral part of any postcolonial narrative. DeLoughrey and Handley in their introduction to *Postcolonial Ecologies* draw insights from Franz Fanon and Edward Said and say "that histories embedded in the land and sea have always provided vital and dynamic methodologies for understanding the transformative impact of empire and the anticolonial epistemologies it tries to suppress." (4) *The Last Wave* chronicles the histories of Andaman Islands nestled in the Indian Ocean, its people and its forests and the transformation they have undergone in the wake of colonial and neo-colonial domination and provides vital episodes to understand the impact of such domination. On one occasion David Bhaskaran was on his crocodile survey when he spots, in a clearing in the mangrove, a group of three people, two locals with a Britisher named Michael Ross. Ross was a journalist and was there to click pictures of naked Jarawa women and sell them to magazines in the West. David accuses Ross: "You, Michael Ross, you bloody Britishers screwed these people—now what are you taking pictures for?" . . . An angry Ross retaliates, proving the narrator's point, "Who is screwing the Jarawas now? Actually screwing them? For a thousand quid—your fellow Indians . . . will get you two nights with a Jarawa woman. Britishers don't come and screw them. Your fellow fucking Indians do" (147). The dialogue between David and Ross is a clear indicator that the voiceless Jarawa people are victims of sexual exploitation by the dominant groups. They are victims of a wider global imperial capitalist design. It gives the reader inkling to the operation of colonial matrices of power which is instrumental in subjection of the Jarawa and the Andaman Islands.

Major postcolonial theorists like Franz Fanon and Homi Bhabha have analyzed the "colonized consciousness, the subjectivity of the individual within a culturally, linguistically, and economically occupied nation or region whose selfhood is a site both of occupation and response", writes Donald Hall in *Subjectivity* (114-115). In the appendix of the novel "The Jarawas: a Historical sketch" (283-286) Sekhsaria gives a detailed chronology of the colonization of Andaman Islands. We are told that it was first in 1789 that the British East India Company "decides to set up colony in the Andaman Islands; Lt Hyde Colebrooke visits the islands, meets native islanders and records some of their language . . . the colony that was set up was abandoned a few years later" (283) We learn that after the sepoy mutiny of 1857, the British sent the mutineers and criminals to the islands and established penal settlement, known commonly as Kalapani or deportation to the dark waters in 1858. 1869 records the earliest evidence of timber extraction from the Andaman forests by the British. Later in 1896 they built the infamous Cellular Jail and established the Karen village of Webi on Middle Andaman Islands (284). Occupation of land in the islands began when the prisoners who had served their term or otherwise behaved themselves properly were released and some land was given to them to live in and begin a new life. The others who came to settle in the islands were the wandering Bhantus, who were constantly being "implicated and regularly persecuted for being thugs and dacoits." (21) Also many families from Burma, especially the Karens and Mopahs, and the labour force brought in from mainland India to help the British in timber extraction and building the Andaman Trunk Road settled in various parts of the Islands encroaching upon Jarawa territory. Sekhsaria notes with concern that a Jarawa tribal reserve was finally established by the Government of India in 1957 with an objective to protect the Jarawa inside the 1000sq km reserve and to prevent settlers from encroaching upon it, "today, there are only about 250 of them and vast expanses of their rainforest homelands have been cleared to accommodate settlers and to feed the huge timber industry on which rests the economic foundation of the Andamans" (*Islands in Flux* 60).

Andaman Islands with their huge untapped economic resources are a neo-colonial capitalist's paradise. Giving a post-colonial critique of domination, Ranjit Guha in his book *Dominance without Hegemony: History and Power in Colonial India*, discusses capital's tendency to universalize and exploit. He says that this "tendency derives from the self-expansion of capital. Its function is to create a world market, subjugate all antecedent modes of production, and replace jural and institutional concomitants of such modes and generally the entire edifice of precapitalist cultures by laws, institutions, values and other elements of a culture appropriate to bourgeois rule" (13-14). Capitalism, one of the colonial matrices of power and subjection produces subjectivity, in this case Jarawa subjectivity.

The universalized capitalism that has invaded the Andamans has replaced indigenous Jarawa culture not only by restricting their habitat but also by appropriating their ancient knowledge of leading a self-sufficient healthy life and by entrapping them with gifts and modern ways of life. The Jarawa had a unique way of honey extraction without harming the bees. They "used the leaves of a plant called tomale, the juice of which worked as a bee-intoxicant. 'After applying the juice to their bare bodies, they scamper up huge trees like monkeys . . . Tomale juice has an unbelievable effect on the bees. They get drowsy and . . . lose all their aggression and all orientation . . . they don't sting. You can easily get all the honey you want. It is simple and efficient method and completely riskfree" (*The Last Wave* 148). But the amount of honey gathered in this manner could not cater to the global demand for honey, therefore, modern modes of production of natural resources were introduced and imposed which replaced the ancient ecological methods of production and acted as a tool of subjugation.

Chibber discusses the expansion of capitalism and ensnaring the subject into consenting to the rules of capitalism. According to him, "the universalizing process is underway if agents' reproductive strategies shift toward market dependence" (111). In the narrative of *The Last Wave* we find several instances of the Jarawa leaving their hostility and coming out of their forests for gifts of bananas and coconuts from people. As Felix, an immigrant and encroacher, tells Seema that the Jarawa are gradually shedding their hostility and making friendship with the settlers. He says, "There is no more fighting between us like there used to be. . . . They say the Jarawas eat only from the forest and the sea . . . for four years now, we have been giving them cooked rice for which they come here regularly" (142-43). The administration and the local people have been enticing the Jarawas to interact with them with tastes of life and goods available outside the forest so that they become materially dependent on them. Referring to Tanumei, a Jarawa youth, who had been treated for fracture in his leg at the Port Blair hospital, Felix recounts an encounter, "[Tanumei] returned from Port Blair and started behaving like a hero; maybe they showed him too many of our films there. He came here a few months ago with a group of four and asked for rice. He wanted the aluminium vessel too."I want the degchi, "he kept saying" (149). Felix's argument reinforces the point that the capitalist class bases its rule on consent. Chibber analyzes Dipesh Chakrabarthy's discourse on Indian capitalism where Chakrabarty is of the opinion that "what makes Indian capitalism generate such forms of power is its specifically *colonial* character" (111). Chibber cites Chakrabarty's argument in this regard from his book *Rethinking Working-*

Class History: "[T]he manager's authority was *essentially colonial*. It derived more from the colonial situation than from any other factor internal to the production process . . . The Scottish manager in a Calcutta jute mill was something he could never have been at home" (111-12). Phenomena peculiar to colonial capitalism is "arbitrary power, the use of terror, the mobilization of traditional hierarchies, the creation of debt obligations—the multifaceted reliance on interpersonal power" (112) which perform the narrative of political and economic modernization and push the Jarawas to a subjective position. David Bhaskaran's recounting of his dialogue with an anthropologist working with the Tribal Welfare Department further reiterates the neocolonial dynamic of power in the Andaman Islands: "if there is one thing that screwed up the Jarawa, it was these contact parties. These were indeed parties where the main aim of the men who came . . . was to have fun and to make contact with the Jarawa women, literally. They'd boast of how many women they touched and where . . . 'What friendship David?' he said, 'You drop gifts and they pick them up. It's like throwing grain and then waiting to snare the birds. The Jarawas got snared, David. They lost their freedom forever.'" (137)

The people from the mainland were colonized subjects brought by force to the islands who, as Fanon argues in his book *Black Skin, White Masks,* suffer from an "inferiority complex" (Fanon, 18). The inferiority complex created in the colonial subjects complicates their relationship with others, whereby, they disalienate themselves from the colonial ideology and continue with it in order "to scrutinize the self . . . to touch the other, to feel the other, to explain the other to myself" (231). The Andaman Islands and the Jarawa tribe colonized culturally, linguistically, and economically by the settlers who had a colonized consciousness became the site of occupation and response, exemplifying a typical ambivalence of the colonized consciousness. Stjepan Mestrovic notes that the "human agents do create knowledgeable and meaningful representations of the world in their quest for what might be termed agency, but they are also driven by powerful and often hidden and mysterious passions" (qtd. Hall 124). Discussing the psychology of subjectivity Judith Butler in her book *The Psychic Life of Power: Theories in Subjection* writes: "If the conditions of power are to persist, they must be reiterated; the subject is precisely the site of such reiteration, a repetition that is never merely mechanical" (16). In the condition of postcoloniality the Indian subject reiterate and extend the colonial oppression that they suffered and further it by enacting the capitalist power dynamic in the Andamans.

The settlers by way of explaining the difference between themselves and the original inhabitants considered the aboriginal people of the island, the Great Andamanese, the Onges and the Jarawas, as the uncivilized 'other' who needed to be civilized and the land that they had usurped was their own. Felix, one such settler, brought into the island as a forest labour, settled illegally in the Jarawa reserve, talks to Seema, one of the researchers in the novel, *The Last Wave*. He justifies his claim to the land, "'we created the settlement with our sweat and blood. We cleared the forest, prepared the fields, constructed our houses; . . . Maybe this was Jarawa territory. *Was*,' he stressed. But *now*, it is ours. This is our land. Earlier, for all these years we had to fight the Jarawas.' . . . 'We can even make these junglees human. We'll civilize them.' . . . 'See in other areas, these fellows these Jarawas are still aggressive, but when they come here, they know who the boss is. They listen to us. They know how to behave" (142-43). Here, Felix is enacting the role of the colonizer out to civilize the other, to control the other, to feel the other and to explain the other to himself. The Jarawas are unaware of the political and capitalist agenda of the colonizer of encroaching into their territory and usurping their resources. According to Ania Loomba "colonization was the *cause* which engendered psychic difference along racial lines and annihilated the black subject into nothingness." (143) Construction of Jarawa people as the junglee 'other' who need to be civilized literally annihilates them into nothingness. They are denuded of agency.

In an episode in the novel, the Jarawas kill and mutilate the body of a police inspector, Inspector Pillai, in Tirur, to avenge the honour of one of their women on whom Pillai had forced himself. This incident is projected as a murderous and barbaric act of the Jarawas. The news reports are full of the killings and the brutalities of the Jarawas. Harish, another researcher, reflects on this and gets a spontaneous response from a local named Ram Krishna "The Jarawas didn't publish that newspaper, did they? Who asks them anyway?" (95) Neither the atrocities of the colonizer, nor the reality of the suffering colonized is ever foregrounded. The version of the Jarawas in this case would never be heard since they have no agency. This is a clear example of Spivak's argument how subjectivity itself has been colonized. In "Can the Subaltern Speak?" she points out that any attempt to recover the voices, perspectives, and subjectivities of the socially outcast and the illiterate (the Jarawas in this case) is heavily compromised and possibly doomed. Arguing about the effacement of the subaltern subject and voice-consciousness, Gayatri Spivak holds that, in the texts, such as police reports, that describe these acts, "one cannot put together a 'voice'", only "an immense heterogeneity" (297). The Jarawas, although they sporadically retaliate against perpetrators attacking them with showers of arrows, are invariably left without agency or voiced self-expression. In this context it is relevant to cite the Kenyan writer Ngugi wa Thiong'o's insightful discourse on his incarceration done by a local Kenyan policeman during his detention in 1977 as noted in one of his two memoirs entitled *In the House of the Interpreter*. He narrates this incident in order to emphasize on the "traces of "mental miscegenation" that the imperial system had left behind them before their departure from Africa. By granting apparent "independence" to the natives, in fact the colonizers had opened the floodgates of indirect domination in the form of Neo-colonialism" (Sharma 140). This legacy is also the most perilous and leaves the natives with no agency. Thus, the imperial oppression reflects itself in the atrocities of the police in the case of Thiong'o in Africa as in case of the Jarawas in the Andamans.

David Hall discusses Homi Bhabha's theory of agency where Bhabha argues that "mimicry, hybridity, sly civility . . . this luminal moment of identification—eluding resemblance—produces a subversive of subaltern agency that negotiates its own authority" (115). The Jarawas in fact adopt tactics of survival by leaving their hostility towards the outsiders and accepting gifts and small favours from them. This mask of friendliness and acceptance of oppression is "an instance of performative agency that unsettles, effects change, and ironizes all notions of *real* identity" (115). The Jarawas come in contact with the settlers and contact diseases that they never knew before. Their nakedness is exhibited and sold; they become addicted to tobacco, paan masala and alcohol, which they receive as gifts from the settlers and tourists, and become self destructive. Already marginalized and deprived in their own land they become unable to take responsibility for themselves in spite of mimicking the ways of the colonizers. The process of mimicry becomes subversive and self destructive as the Jarawas fail to negotiate their own space. SK talking to Harish says wistfully that, "The Jarawas . . . are a lost cause anyway. It's too late. The day their hostility went, when that Tanumei fellow was taken to Port Blair and brought back—the Jarawas lost it. They stand no chance now. In some ways, it is the process of evolution" (192). As a result of this, they annihilate themselves to a petty number of 383 people as per the 2011 census (286).

A parallel can be drawn with the Banyamulenge people, an African tribe from Mulenge in the mountains in Congo who were victims of genocide in the Katumba Refugee camp in Burundi in 2004. Nshombo in a post in the *Boise Weekly* writes: "During the First Congo war, the Banyamulenge participated in overthrowing the dictator Mobutu, joining with the Rwandan army, but the Rwandans could not accept them as their compatriots despite facial similarity and speaking the same language. With the war stirring up the Congo and more rebel groups joining in, all the Rwandans had to return to their home country at some point. The Congolese asked the Banyamulenge to go as well. For the Banyamulenge, Mulenge was more than their home; most of them had never been to Rwanda or any other place other than Mulenge. The Rwandan government denounced them for being Congolese while the Congolese claimed that they were but Rwandan. This left them as a people without a nation." (22 May 2009)

Like the Banyamulenge, the Jarawas too are linguistically and spatially limited; they do not know anything beyond life in their rainforest. The loss of their forest is a road to extinction for them. In the context of annihilation of the entire tribe of Great Andamanese Sekhsaria argues that, "the Great Andamanese were on the verge of extinction they did not know was coming; their own battles had long been lost, and here, in the twentieth century they were collaborating with their annihilators, the British", towards the end of the nineteenth century and the beginning of the twentieth century. 'God alone knows what else is going on – it could be a time bomb waiting to explode. The fuse perhaps has already been lit'" (127).

Destruction of Andaman's flora and fauna, corruption of indigenous people by the colonizers and annihilation of complete tribes due to contact with people from the outside world forms the major concern of the novel. Contemporary postcolonial studies interrogate these concerns and raise questions like: where to now in the wake of material development and expansion? This brings us to the pressing concern of subjectivity of nature and her people by the colonizers who rob them of their agency. Subjectivity denotes a social construct and is determined by repression, victimization, lack of opportunity to grow. Victimization and subordination of the Jarawas and the Andaman Islands performs itself in the novel, *The Last Wave*.

Works Cited

Butler, Judith. *The Psychic Life of Power: Theories in Subjection*. Stanford University Press, 1997.

Chibber, Vivek. *Postcolonial Theory and the Specter of Capital*. Navayana, 2013.

DeLoughrey, Elizabeth and George Handley, ed. *Postcolonial Ecologies: Literatures of the Environment*. OUP, 2011.

Fanon, Frantz. *Black Skin, White Masks*. Trans. Charles Markmann. Grove Press, 1967.

Guha, Ranajit. *Dominance without Hegemony: History and Power in Colonial India*. Harvard University Press, 1997.

Hall, Donald E. *Subjectivity*. Routledge, 2004.

Loomba, Ania. *Colonialism/ Postcolonialism*. Routledge, 1998.

Nshombo, FBM Fidel. "A people without a Nation" *Boise Weekly*, 22 May 2009. www.boiseweekly.com/TheGrip/archives/ 2009/05/22/ a-people-without-a-nation

Sekhsaria, Pankaj *Islands in Flux: The Andaman and Nicobar Story*. Harper Litmus, 2017.

_____. *The Last Wave: An Island Novel*. Harper Collins, 2014.

Sharma, Paulomi. "Examining the Politics of Female Identity and Ethnicity in Ngugi wa Thiong'o." *PostScriptum* July 2018 postscriptum.co.in/wp-content/uploads/2018/07/pS3.iiPaulomi.pdf

Spivak, Gayatri Chakravorty. "Can the Subaltern Speak?" *Marxism and the Interpretation of Culture*, ed. Cary Nelson and Lawrence Grossberg. University of Illinois Press, 1988.

A Feminist Reading of Selected Indigenous and Tribal Narratives from Rajasthan

JAGRITI UPADHYAYA

Folk tales, song and ballads are repositories of the communal consciousness of a society or culture at a given point of time and are rich carriers of meaning continued in the oral tradition. Tribal and indigenous literatures form a rich repertoire in the oral tradition which now is being written, translated and anthologized. Replete with tropes and metaphors, most of them from mythical traditions, these not only trace narratives of cultural traditions and conventions but also subvert and explode social hierarchies, structures and forms and question societal mores and norms.

Rajasthan has a number of indigenous tribes like the Bhils, the Kalbelias, the Langas, the Manganiyars, the Mers, the Meenas, the Thoris inhabiting the various parts of the state right from the desert of Thar to the jungles of Banswara. Their rich literary tradition is representative of its own cultural praxis and an atavistic communal consciousness, and used in multilayered symbolic forms to convey simple practices of the household to complex intertextuality of tales where the divine and the earthly come together at times with supernatural creatures to convey the deeper philosophical meanings of life. These tales also reflect a close affinity with Mother Nature that ecologists like Arne Naess would say, implies 'bio centric equality.'

My paper would explore how women are positioned in certain indigenous and tribal literature through select stories (in English translation) and how they centralize the marginalized feminist concerns. The story of Dhinga Ganwar, in which the Goddess Parvati takes the form of a Bhil woman to go and meet her paramour, traces the Naata Pratha in which a married woman can have sexual liaison with another man or may even choose to go and live with him without fear of ostracization or social ridicule. Jasma of the Odhs traces the undaunted courage of an Odh woman who challenges the all-powerful feudal King to save her honour, while 'Dohri Joon' by Nobel nominee Vijay Dan Detha narrates the story of lesbian love which transcends biological bodies and challenges the heterosexual matrix.

These stories challenge not only the hegemony of the patriarchal paradigms but also undermine the societal gender dualism by articulating what is termed 'aberrant' in heteronormative binaries. Therefore these narratives break stereotypes, deconstruct the meanings ascribed by hegemonic discourses and legitimize the concerns of the 'Other' by foregrounding their voices, at times playfully, at times polemically. They usurp the status quo, subvert institutional and systemic oppression and endorse their own representable space.

Feminist theories recognize the inherent inadequacy of male-created ideas of hegemony and male dominance and seek to recognize the struggle of women for social, economic, political, racial, and gender equality. They aim to give voice to the mute, stifled, oppressed and often silenced voices of women. The folk stories chosen here are from the collection titled *Manzhal Raat* by Rani Laxmi Kumari Chundawat and its translation by Kamini Dinesh and are analyzed from a feminist point of view.

Cultural Feminism celebrates women's special qualities, women's ways and women's experiences and shapes their stories and their vicissitudes in ways different from those of men. Women's stories locate women's cultures, women's way of seeing; they designate meaning to women's voices and make women's consciousness visible to us. In *Tapestries of Life*, Bettina Apthekar contends that women try to find a meaning in their daily activities even when their lives are fragmented, dispersed and episodic.

A Eurocentric liberal feminist perspective focuses on how women take up cudgels against a dominating male culture and subvert the patriarchy while in the folk stories of Rani Laxmi Kumari Chundawat we find that women defy male hegemony while maintaining their traditional roles as wives, daughters, mothers, sisters or even paramours.

The story of Jasma explores how a woman from a low caste community, of the Odhs, traditionally mud-diggers and earlier a nomadic tribe, defies the powerful ruler Rao Khangar who falls in love with the beautiful, married Jasma when he espies her working at the site of a pond being dug in his kingdom. He tries to win her over by using temptation, coercion and even underhand means but the virtuous Jasma is not swayed. Khangar's thoughts about her are full of lust and desire; he compares her matchless beauty to those of the divine nymphs, the Apsaras and tells himself: "This peerless gem has not been created by the Almighty to live in a poor labourer's hut, she should adorn the palace of a king." (Dinesh 4)

Such are the thoughts of a feudal king for whom women are either objects of desire to be subjected to the whims and fancies of a ruler or ornamental trophies to glamourize their palaces; and they would not refrain from coveting even the lawful wives of their hapless subjects. Sarah Grimke in "Letters on the Equality of the Sexes" says, "Man has subjugated woman to his will, used her as a means to promote his selfish gratification, to minister to his sensual pleasure, to be instrumental in promoting his comfort, but never has he desired her to elevate herself to that rank she was created to fill" (Bhatnagar 48).

When Jasma with pots of water on her head is moving towards her hut Khangar addresses her thus:

Your sovereign calls you, O Jasma of the Odhs,

> Come, see the royal palace, O Jasma of the Odhs,
> O maiden saffron skinned, O beauty so tender and slim,
> He has lost his heart to you, the Rao Khangar. (Dinesh 5)

Jasma is startled and taken aback. The King! She shakes like a leaf. Then composing herself she folds her hands and replies:

> Why should I look at your palace, O fond King, (wayward King)
> Happy am I in the lowly thatch that is my home. (*Ibid.*)

Rao Khangar persists in his entreaties to her trying to win her over with all temptations possible, inviting her to visit his queens, his princes, but Jasma rebukes him saying she is happy amongst her poor kinsmen. The Rao, inebriated with her beauty, blocks her path saying:

> You have pleased me, woman and be it known to you,
> He has lost his heart to you the Rao Khangar. (*Ibid.*)

Furious, Jasma retorts:

> O King, who wrongs his people,
> What care I for your queens.
> O Rao, intent on corrupting his people,
> He has gone astray, the Rao Khangar.

In his lustful desire for Jasma the Rao forgets that his duty lies in safeguarding his subjects. He is as unruly as his desire and conscious only of his might: "unbridled are the misdeeds of the wayward monarch. When wealth, youth and unbridled power are compounded with indiscretion." (*Ibid.*7)

Kate Millett in *Sexual Politics* draws an analogy between race and sexual domination of males and stresses that "the relationship between the races is indeed a political one which involves the general control of one collectivity, defined by birth, over another collectivity, also defined by birth." (Gilbert and Gubar 337). Referring to the oppression of the subordinated race and inadequate redress through political institutions Millett opines, "Quite in the same manner, a disinterested examination of our system of sexual relationship must point out that the situation between the sexes now and throughout history, is a case of that phenomenon Max Weber defined as *herrschaft*, a relationship of dominance and subordinance. What goes largely unexamined, often even unacknowledged (yet is institutionalized nonetheless) in our social order, is the birthright priority whereby males rule females. Through this system a most ingenious form of 'interior colonization' has been achieved. . . . However muted its present appearance may be, sexual dominion obtains nevertheless as perhaps the most pervasive ideology of our culture and provides its most fundamental concept of power." (Gilbert and Gubar 338)

Impassioned and maddened by his desire Khangar still pursues Jasma threatening to kill her husband and her brothers-in-law. Undeterred, Jasma defies him ferociously like a lioness, stamping her feet and looking at him angrily when he tries to grab her hand: "She chose to work hard all day to earn her livelihood rather than to live in the zenana of a king. How base and vile were the comforts of the palace obtained at the cost of adulterous infidelity. Life in the lowly thatched hut was happier." In spite of all inducements Rao Khangar fails to lure Jasma away from the path of virtue. In acerbic language she retorts: "You are our sovereign. Is it not sinful to covet your subject's wife? Are you not ashamed of yourself, O ill-begotten King! Be guided by reason." (Dinesh 8) Her whole body shakes with uncontrollable anger. Here is the portrayal of a truly courageous woman who chooses to fight back even the ruler who was the mightier of the two. Khangar in his infatuation does not understand her unfailing devotion to and her unwavering love for her dark-skinned, poor labourer husband. Rao Khangar assuming that Jasma is afraid of her menfolk tells her, "Say but the word and the lord of your house shall die O Jasma!" And as he holds her hand, her anger flares up. Pushing him away with all her might she defies him thus, "I will break your skull and dash your brains out and then die myself, if you take one step forward, roared Jasma. . . . The fiery ardour of the chaste wife surpasses even the splendid brilliance of the mighty sun." (Dinesh 9)

The next day the tents of the Odhs are nowhere to be found. Khangar is furious. Outraged, that a mere woman from a low community had the intrepidity and audacity to outdo him, he orders his men to bring Jasma to him, "Persuade her, force her, abduct her what you will, but bring her to me at any cost." The men set out in pursuit; seeing their horses Jasma trembles. Rather than bring death and destruction to her hapless tribe and dishonour to herself by surrendering to the iniquitous lust of the Rao, she valiantly chooses to immolate herself. "What is this life worth, if the honour and sanctity of a wife's devotion is violated? Is it not better to die?" (Dinesh 10)

When Khangar arrives there Jasma is already aflame. Thus Jasma comes across as a true fighter, a courageous votary of women's dignity and honour, who through sheer undaunted valour challenges corrupt power systems and an exploitative feudal system.

The second story is an inherent part of the folk culture of Rajasthan and is about the female deity the 'Dhinga Gavar.' The festival of Gangaur begins the next day of Holi and is celebrated with much fanfare in the traditional worship of Shiva (Gan) and his consort, the goddess Parvati (Gauri). Married women and newly-wed brides fast and perform the required rituals for a happy conjugal life and the longevity of their husbands and unmarried girls worship the Gangaur for a husband of their dreams.

Dressed in their finery, bedecked with jewels the women fast and pray to Isar (Shiva) and Gangaur (Parvati) for marital bliss. The celebration lasts for sixteen days and on the final day a huge procession of the Gavar is taken through the main streets of the city with much celebration and public participation and the Gangaur who has come to her parents' house is sent back to her husband's place.

The story of Dhinga Gavar is a little different. In the oral indigenous tradition it is said that Shiva once dressed himself up as a cobbler to tease Parvati. Not to be left behind, his consort dresses up as a Bhil tribal woman and goes to the cobbler in the darkness of the night as part of a tradition followed by certain tribes known as the 'Naata Pratha.' The Naata involves the acceptance of a woman living with a man as his spouse without the ceremony of marriage. It can be practised by widows, or women physically abused by their husbands or women separated from their husbands. These women are not termed as morally degraded or sinful or bad nor are they treated as social pariahs to be pushed to the margins. The children born of such a relation enjoy all societal and inheritance rights in these tribal societies. Simone de Beauvoir in her iconic work *The Second Sex* contends, "Marital fidelity in our civilization, where patriarchal traditions survive, still seems much more heinous for the wife than for the husband." (565) Simone argues that woman's adultery defrauds the husband of his legitimate heirs and therefore he treats his wife as his property and perpetuates the prohibitions surrounding her by keeping her in a state of dependency: "She frequently interiorizes them; she closes her eyes to her husband's marital vagaries, though her religion, her morality, her 'virtue,' forbid the same behaviour on her part' (565). In a country driven so much by its insistence on a female's fidelity to one man and the taboos associated with her chastity such a liaison through the 'Naata' is revolutionary and explodes the typical orthodox patriarchal system and critiques the hypocritical moral stance of its people.

The Dhinga Gavar celebrations start on Teej and the idol of Gangaur is put on a pedestal at different places in the city but without the idol of Isarji beside her. Even widows are permitted to worship her and the concept of the goddess doing the 'Naata' provides it a sort of social legitimacy.

The third story is 'Dohri Joon' in Volume XIII of *Baatan ri Phulwari* by the Nobel nominee and path-breaking folklorist Vijay Dan Detha, fondly called Bijji, is about same-sex love between two rural women, narrated evocatively and erotically. In 1973 the concept of 'woman identified woman' was an important lesbian concept which focused on the lesbian as one who believed in the primacy of women and saw the lesbian as a source of an alternative model of female identity and not simply a choice of sexual activity. Says Peter Barry in *Lesbian/ Gay criticism in Beginning Theory*: "The lesbian feminist position identified in this essay makes lesbianism central to feminism, since lesbianism turns away from various forms of collusion with patriarchal exploitation and instead consists of relationships among women which, by definition, constitute a form of resistance to, and a radical reorganizing of, existing forms of social relations" (136).

In *The Straight Mind and Other Essays*, Monique Witting does not consider lesbians as women because for her the word 'woman' carries with it too many constructions and associations. She states, "Lesbianism is the only concept I know of which is beyond the categories of sex (woman and man), because the designated subject (lesbian) is not a woman, either economically, or politically, or ideologically. For what makes a woman is a specific social relation to a man, a relation that we have previously called servitude, a relation which implies a personal and physical obligation as well as economic obligation . . . a relation which lesbians escape by refusing to become or to stay heterosexual' (32).

Detha's story begins innocuously like a fable, "Once upon a time there were two villages situated at a distance of forty-eight miles from each other. There lived two baniya Seths famous throughout the land for their stinginess but were inseparable friends. And as fate decreed they married on the same auspicious day, their beautiful wives conceive at the same time and so they promise each other that if one had a son and the other's wife bore him a daughter, then the two children would be married to each other when they grow up. But nature wills otherwise and the two wives give birth to a daughter each under the same auspicious planet and the same astrological juncture. One of the Seths, out of greed of future dowry and under pressure to be true to his word, tampers with the truth and announces the birth of a boy by getting the brass-plate sounded loudly and proudly. Initially his wife presumes it to be a joke but the Seth raises his daughter like a boy, dressing her in a dhoti, angarkhi and pugree. His daughter's youthful bloom at puberty also doesn't deter him. His wife tries to reason with him and dissuade him from deceiving others but the obstinate Seth is not willing to listen to her. The daughter reaches marriageable age and the Seth makes ready for getting his 'son' married to his friend's, the other Seth's, daughter. He brusquely dismisses his wife's argument that a girl cannot be married off to another girl, saying that he had already fixed the marriage when the child was in the womb of its mother. When his goodly wife objects he retorts: "what's in a marriage? He answered. 'It's just a ceremony to be performed, but a promise I've given can't be broken till death."

A stunned wife tries to bring her husband to his senses arguing that nature had given them a daughter and how could his promise be fulfilled through what she lacked physically. The husband said, "I never do things in half measures. I will lead my son's marriage party with pomp and show. We will get a fabulous dowry. A man doesn't go back on his word. Why should I suffer a loss for what is nature's fault?" When questioned by the wife as to how would the daughter cope with the lack of marital fulfillment in bed the Seth replies confidently that wise women find ways of impregnating their wombs in the absence of husbands away from home for long periods of time, or with impotent husbands and in a caustic tone reminds her that she too is the child, not of her mother's husband, but of the local shoemaker and still he had condescended to marry her.

The daughter, nurtured as a son, is innocently oblivious to the concept of biological sex, behaves like a boy and hopefully awaits the appearance of the masculine moustache so she could twirl it in the fashion that men do and is overjoyed at the prospect of her marriage to a the daughter of the other Seth. A friend catches sight of her while she is bathing and lays bare the travesty before her but the Seth's daughter refuses to believe her and tells her that she would marry the other girl because marriage for her is a union of two hearts.

After the wedding with much fanfare, the bride and the groom, mesmerized by each other's beauty, spend two nights just gazing at each other and singing encomiums of the other's pulchritude. On the third night, the groom at the insistence of his shy bride removes his angarkhi and the bride on finding her husband to be a woman just like her, is stunned into immobility. "The bride looked down at his newly bared chest, and before she realized what she was doing she started screaming, and then fell down on the bed in a heap. Half-conscious, she mumbled, "You are a woman! What kind of revenge is being sought from a previous life?" (Merrill 149). The puzzled groom removes the clothing of the bride only to face the reality with a bitter shock. His illusion is shattered and so is his happiness. Contrite with remorse the groom brings the bride to consciousness and begging her forgiveness asks her to punish him in whatever way the bride thought fit. The wise bride on getting to know how the Seth had woven a web of delusion to keep his pride and his greed for dowry, and of her husband's innocence tells him that he has been more wronged than she. Taking an equal blame herself she tells him that they would now sink or swim together. The bride said soothingly, "Nothing has been ruined yet. We'll just have to find a path of happiness that's our very own. I mean there's nothing special in a man and a woman getting married. Watch the sun rise in the east every day, and it's wonderful. But if it were to rise in the west one morning, now that would be something to talk about." (Merrill151).

Dressing the groom as a girl in all her wedding finery and jewellery from her trousseau she names him Teeja and herself Beeja and, in spite of the Seth's insults and threats, they both leave the house to embark on their own journey together. "The village elders too take umbrage, saying: 'If a woman marries another woman, what is a man to do—go and find a mouse hole for himself?'" (Vanita, Ch. 52). Beeja brings a scarecrow dressed in a pugree, angarkhi, dhoti and with an impressive moustache under a bulbous nose. Telling the menfolk that they are no better than a scarecrow, which would least terrify them, the two girls walk away undeterred. In front of them is nature in all its lush greenery. Says the story-teller, "The beauty of this earth lay before them, limitless, stretching out in all direction. For the first time, these beloved daughters of nature met with nature. Leaping like doves, they climbed a hill. Mad with joy, they chased each other to the highest peak and began to whirl round and round, holding hands." (Vanita, Ch. 52)

Says the storyteller, "The lovers came together like velvety red birbahuti bugs and lost themselves in an embrace, drinking in the ambrosia of each other's lips as if they could flow into one another. As the rains pent up in the clouds released themselves, so did their ardour gradually slacken. The hillside's lifeless existence had suddenly been rendered vibrant and meaningful. Now there was a new spark in the flash of the lightning." (Merrill 158). Even nature rejoices in and celebrates their love. They frolic in the rain and feel like flowers fluttering and the cup of their joy overflows. The earth unravels its beauty partaking of the beauty of their pure love. (Bhasin 72)

Redefining the concept of heterosexual love Detha questions the mores of marriage, "When they reached the plains they had experienced the height of their passion. If there was anything more pure and more sacred in the world than the clear water shed by the clouds, it was their intense love.'

In another instance when they embrace each other, Teeja saying that her sweet breath would be enough to make Beeja feel better after the filth of the village, we can trace an example of the literary device of 'pathetic fallacy' once again, "the peacocks began to coo and do their elegant mujra courtesies."

The story now brings in the supernatural as is wont in the oral traditions. The two arrive at a deserted well inhabited by a hundred and twenty eight ghosts and it is the chieftain of these ghosts, who tells them that he has witnessed everything that had taken place and he has been responsible for the spectacle of the scarecrow. The ghost chieftain is so touched by their pure, unadulterated love that he feels grateful to them and tells them that he is indeed blessed to witness their love for each other. (Bhasin 74)

He further offers to erect a single-pillared palace for them that would be so majestic that kings would be envious of them because witnessing their pure love has made his life worthwhile. . . . And only women would be able to access the palace, males would be forbidden to even set their eyes on it. With the gentle light of the moon shimmering on the palace and a lotus flower for a bed with rose petals for a bedspread, Teeja and Beeja are lost in a trance of their love. (Bhasin 74)

"Like two love-birds bathed in hues brighter than the vermilion red, they were so engrossed in sheer sensual bliss that they completely forgot about the affairs of the outside world. What could compare with this primeval dance of Kamdev?"

Judith Butler in *Gender Trouble: Feminism and the Subversion of Identity* argues that sex male/ female is seen to cause gender which she classifies as masculine/ feminine which leads to the arousal of desire towards the other gender. She rejects the idea of any connections between gender and desire and finds them flexible and free floating. She says, "There is no gender identity behind the expression of gender. . . . Identity is performatively constituted by the very 'expressions' that are said to be its results." (25)

A fortnight later they visit the village but there is no remonstrance from the villagers as they are all scared of the ghost chieftain. Beeja's mother and a cousin visit them and the cousin relates her tale of woe of an impotent husband and how her father-in-law and brothers-in law rape her. The ghost chieftain offers to set things right for her and uses his power to make her husband sexually virile. This gives Beeja the idea that she could repent for her sin and she too could enjoy conjugal bliss as a man, and rectify the deception practiced on Teeja. The ghost agrees, also granting him the boon to undo his manhood if Beeja so desired. Throughout the night, like two beautiful flamingoes entwined they have their fill of unending pleasure. The next day finds Beeja as a full-bodied man, with a twirling moustache as well and here Detha takes a dig at the Rajasthani menfolk because they find pride and pleasure in their moustache which they twirl to intimidate others. Initially the handsome husband with his curved moustache and his muscular body mesmerizes the wife and Beeja too sings panegyrics of Teeja's voluptuous body and lustrous eyes and their love making is insatiable but a new feeling enters Beeja's mind that as a man he had unlimited powers and a woman's fragility could in no way compare with that. He now starts questioning Teeja and this male dominance of Beeja shatters the egalitarian status of the two because he becomes demanding, aggressive and even turns violent when he finds desirous of establishing his hegemony as the master of the palace, he humiliates and insults Teeja, who baffled by her Beeja's changed behavior, who heretofore had been her beloved paramour, cannot accept the fact that they are not equals. When Teeja asks him to let the ghost chieftain settle the matter as to who owned the palace the infuriated Beeja grows mad with anger, 'Don't think I will be cowed down by this lover of yours,' he shouted. 'I'll establish my own kingdom. I'll collect unlimited hoards of treasure and prepare a huge army. I'll build a mighty fortress and hundreds of queens like you will wait on me in the women's quarters." (Vanita, Ch.52).

In a patriarchal culture the position of a woman is always subordinate to that of a man. She is not supposed to have an individual voice or personality. Her identity lies in that of her husband and consequently she must concede to him in all matters. Wendy Doniger, the eminent Indologist in her translation of the laws laid down by the Indian law-giver in ancient India, Manu, in *The Laws of Manu*, quotes him thus in chapter 9, "(2) Men must make their wives dependent day and night, and keep under their own control those who are attached to sensory objects. (3) Her father guards her in her childhood, her husband guards her in her youth, and her sons guard her in old age. A woman is not fit for independence" (Doniger 197). And a married woman not living with her husband becomes an outcaste, a pariah, ostracized and demeaned, facing insults and malicious canards and treated worse than a leper.

Detha here brings in the oppressiveness that marriage entails and underscores a critique of the sacred institution of marriage in our society.

Beeja even hits her, tugs at her hair, drags her, and shouting and ranting at her even calls her a whore. Teeja finds this rift agonizing and realizes, 'It was the same age-old, well-trodden path. Walking on this would amount to getting into the same rut. As soon as Beeja got into the being as a man, her pure self had blackened, just like darkness envelopes everything after sunset."His forcing himself on her made Teeja feel suffocated and she went became unconsciousness. Their love-making as two women was like manna from heaven but the moment it became heterosexual it became bitter as gall. Meanwhile Beeja goes out and wanders in the jungle like one deranged. Nature seems to him colourless and even the creation seems to be mourning.

Seeking for the eternal oneness of love, his body throbbed to become a woman again. Transmogrified again, he comes back to the palace, shakes the still unconscious Teeja into consciousness and tells her that he has given up his manhood. Finding Beeja bent over her like a delicate creeper, her face glowing with the same tender love for her Teeja pulls her soft, sensuous body into a tight embrace that hasn't slackened till date.

Bonnie Zimmerman is of the opinion that many critics think that to consider lesbianism as an exclusively sexual phenomenon is not an adequate construction of the lesbian experience historically as well. Zimmerman in her essay 'What Has Never Been: An Overview of Lesbian Feminist Criticism' compares two perspectives on lesbianism –one that insists on desire and carnality as a prerequisite and the other with an expanded meaning, its major proponent being Adrienne Rich, who states Zimmerman, offers a compelling inclusive definition of lesbianism: "I mean the term lesbian continuum to include a range—through each woman's life and throughout history of woman-identified experience; not simply the fact that a woman has had or consciously desired genital experience with another woman. If we expand it to embrace many more forms of primary intensity between and among women, including the sharing of a rich inner life, the bonding against male tyranny, the giving and receiving of practical and political support . . . we begin to grasp breadths of female history and psychology which have lain out of reach as a consequence of limited, mostly clinical, definition of 'lesbianism' (Gilbert and Gubar 552).

Lillian Faderman in her iconic overview, 'Surpassing the Love of Man: Romantic Friendship and Love between Women from the Renaissance to the Present' gives a definition that lies between the inclusive and exclusive definitions of lesbianism. In her words, "Lesbian describes a relationship in which two women's strongest emotions and affections are directed towards each other. Sexual contact may be a part of the relationship to a greater or lesser degree, or it may be entirely absent. By preference the two women spend most of their time together and share most aspects of their lives with each other." (Faderman 17-18).

Detha's story, though not a strident strike for lesbianism, nevertheless, challenges the dominant heteronormative binary and with its rich interweaving of fiction, fantasy, and the fantastic, through the tropes of the folk has subverted male hegemony and patriarchy and used the story to foreground an alternate sexuality and gender equality. He has loosened the categories of gender and has reassigned our received meanings of marriage. . . . The lesbian here defies the male's world, his social hierarchy, his ideology of the feminine, and his definition of woman in Simone de Beauvoir's words as the 'other.' As an allegorical fabulist Detha positions the two women at the centre questioning the grand meta-narratives of male-centric universe. Detha opens up a new critical space in which issues of feminism, gender and sexuality are explored in new ways—what Teresa de Lauretis in 'Sexual Indifference and Lesbian Representation' calls 'a conceptual, representational, erotic space. . . . In which women could address themselves to women.' Monique Witting points out, "We have been compelled in our bodies and in our minds to correspond feature by feature, with the idea of nature that has been established for us." But Detha's Beeja and Teeja challenge this assumption not only by their overt physical passion and sexual desire but also by the sharing of a rich, inner life, the bonding against an avaricious father and a bigoted society and finding bliss together bringing the story out of the constrained, clinical definition of lesbianism.

Charlotte Bunch explains, "The lesbian rejects male sexual/political domination; she defies his world, his social organization, and his definition of her as inferior. Lesbianism puts women first while the society declares the male supreme. Lesbianism threatens male supremacy at its core. When politically conscious and organized, it is central to destroying our sexist, racist, capitalist, imperialist system" (Bunch 83).

Detha's characters are strong rural females, not afraid to express their sexual desires, nor do they suffer from any sort of internalized guilt. Replete with desert flavours, rustic idioms, and a wonderful blend of the humorous and the poignant, this tale has centralized the marginalized through the vocalization of a taboo topic to weave a contemporary issue of queer and feminism by a fabulist, to prove that pure, unadulterated love transcends all biological bodies and societal norms. As Kailash Kabir says, "His stories ridiculed the feudal lord, the moneylender, the king, the patriarch and the gods. Lok Katha was only the motif he used to speak out against satta (establishment)."

Works Cited

Agarwal, Swarnlata. *Rajasthan Ke Lokgeet*, Rajasthan Sahitya Academy, Udaipur, 1967.

Bhasin, Mridul, Kailash Kabir, Vandana R Singh, trans. and ed. *New Life Selected Stories of Vijay Dan Detha*." Penguin. archive.org/stream/NewLifeSelectedStoriesOfVijayDanDetha-English /vijay-dandetha-eng1_djvu.txt.

Bunch, Charlotte. "Lesbians as Revolt", *The Feminist Theory Reader: Local and Global Perspectives*, ed. Carole R. McCann and Kyung Kim Seung. Routledge, New York, 2007.

Bhatnagar, Manmohan K., ed. *Feminist English Literature*. Atlantic, New Delhi, 1999.

Butler, Judith. from *Gender Trouble* in *The Norton Anthology of Theory and Criticism*, ed. Vincent B. Leitch et al, W.W Norton, New York, 2018.

Chundawat, Rani Laxmi Kumari. *Maanzhal Raat*, Rajasthani Granthagar, Jodhpur, 2015.

Detha, Vijay Dan. *Baatan ri Phulwadi*, Volume III, Rajasthani Granthagar, Jodhpur, 2009.

Dinesh, Kamini, trans. *Rani Laxmi Kumari Chundawat's Jasma of the Odhs and Other Tales*, Indian Map Service, Jodhpur, 2010.

Doniger, W & B.K. Smith, trans. *The Laws of Manu*, Penguin, New Delhi, 2007.

Faderman, Lillian. *Surpassing the Love of Man: Romantic Friendship and Love between Women from the Renaissance to the Present,* Harper Paperbacks, New York, 2016.

Zimmerman, Bonnie. "What Has Never Been: An Overview of Lesbian Feminist Criticism", *Feminist Literary Theory and Criticism, A Norton Reader,* ed. Sandra M. Gilbert and Susan Gubar. W.W Norton, New York, 2007.

Merrill, Christi A and Kailash Kabir, trans. *Vijay Dan Detha. Chouboli and Other Stories, Volume II*, Katha, Noida and Fordham University Press, New York, 2012.

McLeod, John. *Beginning Postcolonialism,* Viva Books, New Delhi, 2010.

Vanita, Ruth and Saleem Kidwai, ed. *Same-Sex Love in India, A Literary History*. Penguin, New Delhi, 2000.

Wittig, Monique. *The Straight Mind and Other Essays*. Becon, Boston, 1992.

Relevance of Santhali Literature in Present-Day Translations

ANITA GUA HEMBROM

Sujit Mukherjee in his book, *Translation as Discovery*, says, "The best translation in world literature has occurred when the translator has rendered works from other languages into his own" (16). Santhali literature of the Santhals, one of the adivasi communities belonging to the Proto-astroloid race living in the states of Jharkhand, West Bengal, Bihar, Odisha and Assam, maintains this exclusivity in the face of cross-fertilization of various languages between different discourses. One would find considerable number of texts translated from modern Indian languages (Bengali, Odia, Hindi and even English) into Santhali. But, one hardly comes across any work of translation done from Santhali to English or any other Indian language, thus complying with the idea presented by Mukherjee.

Santhali literature has a complex history of translation dating back to the 1870s that can be divided into two phases: (i) the Christian missionary phase which can be studied in terms of colonialism. It spans from 1867 with the establishment of the first Santhal Mission in Benagaria to 1930s; (ii) the Santhali phase which can be studied in terms of post-colonialism starts mostly after Independence. The reasons behind maintaining such exclusivity by an adivasi community like Santhali attributes to cultural, political and linguistic issues. Concentrating on the two phases of history of translation in Santhali literature I will try to substantiate the various possible reasons behind such an exclusive one-way translation. The reasons roughly relate to the colonial representation of the Santhals by the Christian missionaries and British administrators, the fight for the recognition of Santhali language in the Indian Schedule, belief in the untranslatability of the Santhal culture and language and literature, authorship and last but not the least market of the translated texts.

At the time of the emergence of Santhali literature, that is, during the late nineteenth and early twentieth century, the Christian missionaries played a vital role as they were the early writers of Santhali literature as well as translators. During the time when the missionaries started working among the Santhals, Santhali was still an unwritten language and the majority of the Santhals were illiterate. The Santhali literature came into being with the publication of *Hor Koren Mare Hapram ko Reak Katha* (The Traditions and Institutions of the Santhal) by Rev. L.O. Skrefsrud in the 1887. The kind of literature written during the missionary period was mostly collection and translations of the Santhal oral narratives. Some of the works, mostly translations in English, published during the time were: *Santhal Folk Tales* (1891) by A. Campbell, Cecil Henry Bompas's *Folklore of the Santhal Pargana* (1909), P.O. Bodding's *Chapter on Santhal Folklore* (1924), *Santhal Folktales Vol. 1* (1923), *Vol. 2* (1924), *Vol.3* (1925), *The Tradition and Institutions of Santhals* (1924).

Besides this, Christian texts like The Bible, Gospels were being translated into Santhali. What was happening through the project was the cultural translation of the Santhals and not just literary. They were re-interpreted, re-defined and re-presented to the public in general. They were represented as 'noble savage,' 'half-savage,' in need of civilization (Marx 158). This brings us to the first phase, that is, the colonial representation of the Santhals by the Christian missionaries and British administrators. It can be said that they were engaged in the task of translating the culture of the Santhals and were creating new identities which were quite contrary to what the Santhals had conceived of them for so long. For instance, they equated the Santhal deity,

Lita Godet (Messenger God) as the Satan of the Bible and their religion as 'demonic cult' (Culshaw 125 & Marine and Lyche 283). P.O. Bodding, one of the most noteworthy missionaries working among the Santhals, in his *Santhali-English Dictionary* gave the following meaning of the Santhal deity and first Santhal humans mentioned in the Santhal origin story:

Lita: "the name of a spirit, the same as the *Marang Buru*. The traditions tell that *Lita* presented himself to the first human pair as their grandfather and taught them to brew beer and drink it, while drunk they fell in sin, i.e., had their first sexual intercourse." (141).

Pilchu Haram: "The Santhal name for the first man, Adam." (627).

Pilchu Budhi: "The Santhal name for the first woman, Eve." (627)

In the 1920s, the interpretation of the terms *Bonga* and *Marang Buru* (names of the Santhal deity) was in practice. It is to be noted that the term *Bonga,* used by the Santhals to define something supernatural, was a neutral term with no negative or positive connotation attached to it. It is only "a generic term and connotes invisible, inexplicable, supernatural spiritual forces/ powers" (Hembrom 45). However, the Christian missionaries failing to find an analogy for the term *Bonga* considered it to be rejected and denigrated (45). P.O. Bodding, in his book Studies in *Santhal Medicine and Connected Folklore* (1986), defined *Bonga* as something 'malevolent,' 'who harass humanity' (iii-2). In fact, Boddings's works, especially *Kukli Puthi* (Question Book) published in 1898 is quite vital in bringing out such interpretations.

Though the missionaries succeeded in meeting their evangelic ends, that is, the conversion of the Santhals into Christianity, their politics of translation of the Santhal religion brought about a great damage to the latter. Having no authority over the translated texts the Santhals could not challenge the representation of the self and their religion, thus they were further pushed into the periphery. Also, seldom were they the reader of such texts since during the time majority of them were illiterate. Their role was limited to being narrators, in the source language, for the missionaries and the listeners of the translated version (concepts) in the source language. In the absence of any written record of their religion, folklore etc. the originality and the authenticity of the same was lost in translation as there was hardly any scope of doing a comparative study between the original and the translation or challenging the same.

From the 1930s we see the emergence of quite a number of noteworthy Santhali writers. By this time the missionaries had gradually started to lose control over the literary content and context of Santhali literature. With the spread of education and rise in the political and social consciousness the Santhal writers adopted literature as an apparatus to challenge and reject the colonial representation of them. This can be seen as the beginning of a new phase in the history of Santhali literature, that is, the post-colonial phase dominated by the Santhali writers as the creator and proprietor of the literature. This new phase brings us to the second reason, vis-à-vis, belief in the uniqueness of Santhali language, literature and culture and their fight for the inclusion of Santhali language in the Eighth Schedule of the Indian Constitution.

Bhabha says, "Translation is the performative nature of cultural communication" (228). That is to say, when we translate a text we also engage ourselves in communicating culture from one to the other. The Santhals in general and the writers in particular believe in the idea that it is difficult to translate Santhali texts and culture into English or any other language. They seem to give their consent to Benjamin's idea of "untranslatability" (qtd. in Trivedi 124). Here, I would like to throw light on an incident. The Centre for Comparative Literature, Visva Bharati had decided to undertake a translation project where we would translate the plays of Pandit. Raghunath Murmu, the pioneer of the genre of drama in Santhali literature. He is also the pioneer of

Santhali literature as we know it today, that is, literature in Santhali language, by Santhal writer, for Santhal readers in contrast to the early phase. He had written four plays, *Bidu-Chandan* (1942), *Kherwar Bir* (1944), *Darege Dhan* (1948), *Santhal Hul* (posthumous). His writings have a great significance in Santhali literature and social life since they can be studied in the light of cultural and religious revival of the Santhals, after a long span of misinterpretation and representation in the hands of the Christian missionaries. Our aim was to utilize it solely for academic purpose and offer them as texts under the course on tribal literature. Unfortunately, we were denied the copyright by the members of the Murmu family on the grounds that are quite crucial to translation studies. Their very first question to us was, whether the translation of those texts into English would be able to produce the exact essence of the Santhali language and the texts? They explained their doubts with examples that in Santhali there are different expressions for the word 'sit,' for different animate beings and also for different positions of sitting (Murmu). For example,

the expression *up* is used to describe an animal's sitting;

the expression *tic* is used to describe reptiles' stretching out; and

the expression *durup* is used to describe humans' sitting (Murmu).

For various positions of sitting the Santhali expressions are,

Herpet (to sit for a long time in one position);

Edhe (to sit doing nothing);

Loplopo (to crouch or sit hurdled up);

Cocongot (to sit on heels);

Comcorok (used for animals, to sit on hind legs with front legs straightened) (Campbell 301, 214, 440, 141, 148).

The second question they asked, what if the translator/ translated text fails to convey the exact message, intended by Pandit Murmu, in Santhali and who would be the target readers. The questions and doubts raised by them were genuine to their concern given the importance attached to Pandit Raghunath Murmu in the history of Santhali literature. As said earlier, Pandit Murmu is the pioneer of the genre of drama in Santhali literature and his writings mark the significant transition Santhali literature was going through in the 1940s. His plays challenge the Christian missionaries' understanding of the Santhal religion and culture by dealing with things like religious themes, utilizing Santhal myth, portraying mythical characters, incorporating scenes of dancing and singing that were mostly shunned by the missionaries.

Here, it becomes obvious that the responsibility of the translator is very crucial since the translation has to take place from an adivasi language like Santhali, which is marginalized and kept in the periphery, to a mainstream language. To elaborate my point, I give example of the English translation of Santhali songs by Sitakanta Mahapatra, an eminent Indian poet and critic in Odia as well as English. In his notable book, *Men, Pattern of Dust* (1981), he has translated folksongs of the Santhal, Koya and Ho tribes, dedicated to different festivals and occasions. In one of the songs translated, he has translated the cultural specific term, *tuwa dare,* as 'milk tree' which is the literal translation of the Santhali term. The term *tuwa dare* is a metaphor for the term 'mother,' used philosophically when comparing her role to that of a god. Translating *tuwa dare* simply as 'mother tree' fails to justify the philosophy and importance attached to the term and thus, ails to produce the core essence of the song.

Thus, the questions asked are not just related to the issue of translation but to the broader question of representation in the mainstream society and literature. According to Harish Trivedi, translation is not just a transaction between two languages, but rather a complex negotiation between two cultures (191), and the inability to produce the exact message conveyed by the source author would mean that the readers of the translated texts will conceive the partial message/ knowledge. Anisur Rehman in his essay, "Author Text Translator Reader: The New Indian Context", says, "The act of reading is conscious and political acts. There are vital questions involved in this process like who is the reader of a given text, how that reader approaches that text, and at what point of time" (182).

He further explains it by saying that there are three kinds of texts produced in the whole process—one by the author, other by the translator and yet another by the reader—which raises the theoretical question of the multiplicities of text, authorship and readership. As there are two authors involved, the source language author and the target language author. And ultimately, when the text moves to the readers, it gathers infinite reception both in the source language as well as in the target language (182).

The question of the reader and the translator becomes crucial here. It is always assumed that the readers of the translated text will always be someone who does not belong to the source language community. And if they read the translated text without having the first hand knowledge of that community, he/ she might not be able to acquire the essence and do justice to the community he/ she is reading in translation. And perhaps, the message intended by the source author language will remain lost in the translation. Also, the question arises who will play the role of the translator – whether it will be a Santhal with the knowledge of English or a non-Santhal with knowledge of Santhali? Two different results will emerge on the basis of two different translators.

The translation by a non-Santhal with or without the knowledge of Santhali will result in the production of books like Sitakanta Mahapatra's *Men, Pattern of Dust* and Romesh Mohanty's *Vibrant Breath Pulsates* (2015); the first being the collection of tribal folksongs and the other being the transcreation of *Say Sahned* (2006), a collection of poems by

Damyanti Besra, an eminent Santhali poetess from Odisha. The book, *Vibrant Breath Pulsates*, focuses more on the genius of Dr. Mohanty than on the excellence of Dr. Besra. On the other hand, when a Santhal translator with the knowledge of English is doing the translation he/ she tries to retain the originality of the source language by placing it side by side with the translation in the target language. The example of such book is Siran Murmu's *Dagbaha* (1998), translated as *The Blooms of the Cloud* by Litai Hembrom is, perhaps, the only available book of poems to be translated into English. The poems in Santhali by Murmu and their translation by Hembrom are compiled in the same book, thus, equalizing the importance of both the texts and languages.

One cannot deny the fact that translation has served as a doorstep in Santhali literature through which the modern literary genres like novel has entered in the realm of the latter. The Santhali translation of R. Carstairs's *Harma's Village* (1936) as *Harmawak Ato* (1946) by R.R. Kisku Rapaj was the first instance of translation from other language into Santhali. Also this translation introduced the genre of novel in Santhali literature. Since then number texts from other modern Indian languages has been translated into Santhali. Notable among them are:

i. *Rahla Raybar* (2008) by Sobhanath Beshra, translation of Sanskrit verse-poem *Meghdoot* by Kalidasa;
ii. *Arareyak Serma* (2010) by Damyanti Besra, translation of Odia poems *Shabdara Aakash;*
iii. *Haramba* (2013) by Gangadhar Hansda, translation of Odia novel *Dadibudha* by Gopinath Mohanty;
iv. *Sendra* (2014) by Damyanti Besra, translation of Odia poems *Mrigaya* by Phani Mohanty;
v. *Kant Re Jhorka Tahe Kana* (2013) by Yashoda Murmu, translation of Hindi novel *Deewar Me Ek Khidki Rehti Thi* by Vinod Kumar Shukla;
vi. *Seren Anjle* (2015) by Joba Murmu, translation of Bengali poems *Gitanjali* by Rabindranath Tagore;

vii. *Turuyman Tralghant* (2015) by Gangadhar Hansda, translation of Odia novel *Chhaman Atha Guntha* by Fakir Mohan Senapati;

viii. Horog Chinha Shakuntala (2018) by Sunil Murmu, translation of Sanskrit play *Abhijnan Shaktuntalam* by Kalidasa.

Being myself a Santhal and doing research on the historiography of Santhali literature, I have found out that theoretical and practical critique of translation studies are not the only things prevailing among the Santhals but, the cultural and social prejudices also become the barrier in the process of translation. Another crisis that looms large over the world of Santhali literature is the unavailability of large readers. One of the reasons of such a crisis is the lack of education among half of the Santhal population in general. The other half though well-educated is unable to read and write in Santhali because they either get education in the State language of their domicile or in English. Due to this, there is lack of knowledge of the *Ol-Chiki,* the script of the Santhali language, among the majority of Santhals themselves. This leaves no choice for the scope of Santhali literature but to remain limited to the students of the same and academics. In such a wake, translating Santhali texts into English or any other language would definitely increase the marketability of the translated test and popularize the same but on the other hand, it will implicitly lead to the reduction in the popularity of Santhali texts in the original language. It is so because Santhali texts suffer from dearth of proper process of publication except for the texts published by Sahitya Academy. Most of the Santhali texts are either printed personally by the writers or their family members and sent to selected bookshops that sell books in regional languages. There is hardly any publication house working for the publication and marketing of books as compared to the publication houses of other mainstream literatures. Also the amount of texts published per edition hardly ranges from five hundred to two thousand and seldom is a second or third edition of literary texts published.

From the point of view of a research scholar I firmly believe that translation is one such platform where cultural and literary exchanges can take place across different cultures, language and literature. I also firmly believe that both the source language text and the target language texts should be given due importance without jeopardizing the status of either of the two. Santhali is the only adivasi language recognized by the Constitution of India beside, Bodo. Ever since its birth Santhali literature has managed to create good amount of texts that speaks so much about Santhal history, movements, freedom struggles, experiments with literary genres etc. In an adivasi literature like Santhali, I think, translation can serve as a tool to popularize Santhali literature in its original language. This can be done by compiling the original and the translated texts in a single book. By doing so the Santhali writers, the translators and the publishers can become instrumental in rescuing Santhali from remaining dormant and also help in maintaining a status of its own among the mainstream literatures.

Works Cited

Beshra, Sobhanath, trans. *Meghdoot* by Kalidasa. Jharkhand: Sobhanath Besra, 2008.

Besra, Damyanti, trans. *Shabdara Aakash* by Sitakanta Mahapatra. New Delhi: Sahitya Akademi, 2010.

_____, trans. *Mrigaya* by Phani Mohanty. New Delhi: Sahitya Akademi, 2014.

Bodding, P.O. *Chapter on Santhal Folklore.* Kristiania: A.W. Brogger, 1924.

_____. *Santhal Folktales.* Vol. 1-3. New Delhi: Gyan, 1996.

_____, trans. *Hor Koren Mare Hapram Ko Reak Katha* by L.O. Skrefsrud. New Delhi: Bahumukhi Prakashan, 1994.

_____. *Kuk'li Puthi.* Lucknow: Santhal Mission of the Northern Churches, 1955.

_____. *Studies in Santhal Medicine and Connected Folklore.* Calcutta: Asiatic Society, 1986.

Bompas, Henry Cecil. *Folklore of the Santhal Parganas.* London: David Nutt, 1909.

Campbell, A. *English Santhali Dictionary.* Calcutta: Eastern Books, 1984.

_____. *Santhali English Dictionary.* Pokhuria: Santhal Mission Press, 1988.

_____. *Santhal Folk Tales.* Pokhuria, 1891.

Carrin, Marine and Harald Tambs-Lyche. "The Santhals, Though Unable to Plan For Tomorrow, Should Be Converted By Santhals." *Christian and Missionaries in India Cross-Cultural Communication since 1500.* Ed. Robert Eric Frykenberg. Cambridge: William B. Eerdmans Publishing Company, 2003.

Culshaw, W. J. *Tribal Heritage: A Study of the Santhals.* New Delhi: Gyan Publishing House, 1984.

Hansda, Gangadhar, trans. *Dadibudha* by Gopinath Mohanty. New Delhi: Sahitya Academy, 2013.

_____, trans. *Chhaman Atha Guntha* by Fakir Mohan Senapati. New Delhi: Sahitya Akademi, 2015.

Hembrom, Timothius. "Marang Buru Bonga-Satan Equation a Theological Crime." *Journal of Theology.* Volume 32, Issue 2 (2006): pp 43-54.

Mahapatra, Sitakanta. *Men, Patterns of Dust.* Bhubaneswar: Bookland International, 1981.

Marx, Karl. *Notes on Indian History.* Foreign Languages Publishing House, 1947.

Mukherjee, Sujit. *Translation as Discovery.* Hyderabad: Orient Longman, 2006.

Murmu, Pandit Raghunath. *Bidu-Chandan.* 4th ed. Mayurbhanj: Adibasi Socio-Educational & Cultural Association, 2004.

_____. *Kherwar Bir.* Paschim Medinipur: Marshal Bamber, 2011, Rpt.

_____. *Darege Dhan.* Re Paschim Medinipur: Marshal Bamber, 2011.

_____. *Sidu-Kanhu Santhal Hul.* East Singhbhum: Dulai Printers, 1996.

Murmu, Mn. Siran, *The Blooms of the Cloud*, trans. Litai Hembrom. Calcutta: Adibasi Socio-Educational and Cultural Association, 1998.

Murmu, Yashoda, trans. *Deewar Mein Ek Khidki Rehti Hai* by Vinod Kumar Shukla. New Delhi: Sahitya Akademi, 2015.

Murmu, Joba, trans. *Gitanjali* by Rabindranath Tagore. New Delhi: Sahitya Academy, 2015.

Murmu, Bhimwar. Personal Interview. 30 April 2018.

Rehman, Anisur. "Author Text Translator Reader: The New Indian Context." *Translation and Culture Indian Perspectives*, ed. G.J.V. Prasad. New Delhi: Pencraft International, 2010, pp. 178-187.

Trivedi, Harish. "Translating Culture vs. Cultural Translation", *Translation and Culture Indian Perspectives*, ed. G.J.V. Prasad. pp. 188-99.

Skrefsrud, L.O. *Hor Koren Mare Hapram Ko Reak Katha*. Benagaria, 1887.

Oral Narratives: Cultural Deterioration of the Banjara Tribe in India

B. VIJAYA

This paper sensitizes the change in the cultural practices, especially the present marriage system that deteriorates from 'bride price' to 'dowry' in the Banjara Culture. Banjara is not a caste system but a clan system with certain unique features and value system that makes it distinct from other tribes of India. The present cultural changes that have taken place among the Banjara communities are a result of the close living with the caste stricken Hindu society.

The caste stratified Hindu society in the villages; in the closest towns and cities had their impact on the Banjara community. 'Thanda' is a hamlet of the Banjaras in the villages. The same affinity of the clan is visible in the towns and cities but called with different names like streets or colonies of Banjaras. For instance, even in cities like Hyderabad, the Banjara as a clan are living in places like Nandinagar, Jubilee Hills; Ravindernagar, Tarnaka, Banjara Colony Hyatnagar; Singereni Colony, Hyatnagar; Sanjeevreddy Nagar; Uppal; Bodduppal; Balapur and Ankushapur. Hence, Banjara is an ethnic group with egalitarian value system. This proves the indigenous nature of the community. At this juncture, it is appropriate to recollect the words of G.N. Devy on Indigenous people who are known by different names in different parts of the world:

> Recognized as "Aborigines" in Australia, as "Maori" in New Zealand, as "First Nations" in Canada, a "Indigenous" in the United States, as "Janajatis" in India, or as "Tribes" in anthropology, as

> "Notified communities" in the administrative parlance of many countries, as 'Indigenous people' in the discourse of Human Rights, and as "Adivasis" in the terminology of Asian activists, these variously described communities are far too numerous and dispersed in geographical locations to admit of any single inclusive description. (*Indigeneity* xi)

Banjara is one of the important tribes in India with its multilingual, multicultural and religious diversities. Banjara is a synonymous term for Vanjra, Sukali, Sugali, Lambada, Lamani, Bagigar and Lohar. Banjaras were the caravans carrying goods on bullocks and travelled all over India during the pre-colonial period. 'Goarboli' is the language of the Banjara tribe and it is a language without script. Generally, the linguistic heritage is seen in the form of the written tradition. Several socio-political factors decide the status of a particular group of people and their languages in a multilingual society like India.

The unique knowledge in the oral traditions of the Banjaras is in the form of songs and proverbs. Sometimes in tales and riddles also. Orality is in the form of memory of the elders in different hamlets of the Banjara tribes in India. Most of the time, they are not exposed to reading or writing as there is no Script for the Banjaras. At present, these memories of oral traditions are conveyed to the general public or the researchers in the form of their regional languages.

The Banjaras express their knowledge, wisdom, misery, happiness, social relations and other acts of everyday life in their oral tradition. For instance, 'Dhavalo' is an important cultural wailing of the Banjara brides at the time of their wedding ceremony. It is also a very significant and unique practice of the Banjara tribes that articulates their deep love for parents and relatives of the hamlet. It is not the family of the bride alone who participates in this 'dhavalo' but the entire hamlet, especially women. Through this tradition, the bride expresses her grief in words and wails while leaving the parental home. This is the common practice of the Banjara tribe which starts at least ten days before the marriage. During the departure from the parental home, after the wedding, it is suitable to recollect what Deepa Jyothi has mentioned in her article about the song sung by the Banjara bride:

Bapuvore ahiya!
Aha jo tare betena, kera lara melu karena
Ravana kar rochi. Bapu Ahiya!
Bapuvore mana kanayi, koni sassore
Aja jo sasadena, varano gharena melu karena
Tare chatena kato karale do. Bapu ahiya!
Bapuvore ek das daad, kathi melokoni jako
varano pateyaro, lar hath jhalaeno
jholo den lar rejavu kero
Hase bapu ahiya!

English translation:

Oh! My father. With whom today
You are sending your daughter with?
You haven't ignored me any time
But today you are sending me to somebody's home
You have curbed your mind and stood firm.
You haven't given me leave to spend at relatives' house
Not even for ten days
But today you have given me leave forever
By giving my hand to somebody else
You are bidding farewell to me
You are my dear father.

The song is for the bride's father who has nurtured her from her childhood. Besides the bride's 'Dhavalo,' the banjara woman also does dhavalo whenever they meet their dear ones after a long gap. At this juncture, Anand Mahanand rightly says:

> Songs are powerful medium of expressing one's emotions, history and heritage. They represent the collective memory of the people. Through mythical narratives and legends they remind us of our

forgotten past and glorious history. They also deal with social life and everyday problems faced by the people. These songs could be soothing and appealing. They could be vibrant and full of zest. They are precious not only because they are vehicle of past, social life, knowledge and our cultural heritage, but also because of their aesthetic appeal. We feel so proud that we inherit such a beautiful and enduring resource. There is an urgent need to document them and study them. (84)

The words used in 'dhavalo' are more of situational rather than being abstract. Precisely, they are drawn from the life of a banjara woman. Therefore, songs play a prominent role in the unique cultural expression of the Banjara tribe in India.

In fact, originally, even the Vedas, were part of an oral tradition before they took the form of writing. To that extent most of the Indian knowledge system and culture is still in the form of orality. Having discussed few aspects of the oral narratives of the banjara tribe, it is appropriate to document the six-month wedding ceremony of the tribe and its gradual decline that served as an important element of attracting dowry in modern times.

The traditional attire of the Banjaras is distinct and colourful. Men wear 'dhoti' and 'pagdi' (turban) and women wear 'petia' (skirt) which is very rich in embroidery and 'kanchali' (bodice). 'Karar' is the bride price and not the dowry. 'Karar' would be Rs. 316 in a rich family and Rs. 116 in a poor family in addition to the bullock. The following is the six-month wedding ceremony:

The first month is 'Ghota Ghola.' Ghota Ghola is a liquid form of the jaggery. The bridegroom first reaches the Nayak's house and gives him a Hokka (traditional leafy cigar) to the Nayak and continues to stand in front of him until he is convinced to take him to the bride's family. Twice a day, the bridegroom bathes at wells and canals with the help of the brother-in-law, filled with new pots of water. The first time, bathing is done by standing in the 'kakoti' (a wooden container like thing) and second time bathing is by sitting in the 'kakoti.' The mother-in-law is supposed to cook and serve him fresh and hot food with pure ghee and dal.

In the second month the wedding date is fixed and the wedding pots are decorated with different types of leaves. And this stage is called Vaaya Bhande.

The third month is for the Gooter Gorli. At this stage, the bridegroom offers two goats and celebrates the event in the Thanda. The Nayak of the Thanda joins the celebration and the food is served for the entire clan.

The fourth month is called Chudothi. It is a very important event in the entire marriage process. It is a festival atmosphere at the bride's house in which the bridegroom puts 'chuder baliya' (upper bangles) to the bride. These are different banjara bangles and it has a greater symbolic significance. The chuder baliya stands as a symbol of a married woman. If the upper bangles are removed, it is understood that she is a widow. After fifteen days of chudothi, the bride is seen outside with ghunghat (veil).

The fifth month is the exchange of Moi (a sweet dish). This is between the two families, the bride's and the bridegroom's.

In the last and the sixth month, the bride is sent to her parents-in-laws house.

The above-mentioned stages stand as a unique feature of the Banjara marriage system. But due to fast change of the cultural values, the priests have become a compulsory assistant in the Banjara community unlike the traditional marriage system. In the traditional marriage system of the community, there is no role of a priest in the entire process. But due to the cultural deterioration, the middleman i.e., the priest role plays a prominent role at various occasions in the Banjara community. This has become a status symbol in the rich banjara families and an expensive affair to the poor families of the community. This is surely not the impact of the colonization as the postcolonial critics claim.

The cultural changes that have taken place among the Banjara communities are a result of the close living with the caste stricken Hindu society. Dowry is not part of the Banjara culture. It is borrowed from the mainstream Hindu Society as a mask of modernity. Hence, there is a shift from the equalitarian values of the community from the practice of bride price to dowry resulting in a large number of dowry deaths. Gita Ramaswamy and Bhangya Bhukya rightly observe the egalitarian values and the cultural deterioration of the Banjara tribes as follows:

> As the southern Telangana lambada thandas are located in plain areas and near villages they could not protect their cultural values from the onslaught of Hinduism . . . they have given up their traditional marriage systems. This phenomenon is not marked in the forest agency lambada thandas where they maintain their closed life and egalitarian values. (1497)

Hence, this paper sensitizes the nuances of oral narratives and the reasons for the cultural deterioration of the Banjara tribe in India.

Works Cited

Burrow. "Sanskrit and Pre-Aryan Tribes and Languages" *Collected Papers on Dravidian Linguistics*. Annamalai University. Annamalainagar: 1998.

Devy, G.N., Geoffrey V. Davis and K.K. Chakravarty. *Indigeneity: Culture and Representation*. Orient Blackswan: New Delhi, 2009.

Jyothi, Deepa B. "Dhavalo: The Cultural Wailing of the Lambadas", *Kakatiya Journal of English Studies*, Vol. 34, 2015.

Mahanand, Anand. *Oral Traditions of the Indian Tribe*. New Delhi: Author's Press, 2018.

Ramaswamy, Gita and Bhangya Bhukya. "Changing Cultural Patterns of the Lambadas" *Economic and Political Weekly*, Vol. 37, No.16.

“We are not Showpieces”: The Unheard Voices of the *Kanikkar* Tribes of Agasthyarkoodam

ANJU P.S.

Agasthyarkoodam, popularly known as Agasthyamala or Pothigai malai is situated in the southernmost part of Western Ghats within the Neyyar wildlife sanctuary. It lies in the Kerala-Tamil Nadu border with a height of 1868 metre, extended to the five districts of Thiruvananthapuram, Kollam and Pathanamthitta of Kerala; and Tirunelveli and Kanyakumari districts of Tamil Nadu. Agasthyarkoodam biosphere reserve consists of 16 biological hotspots, 1000 species of flowering plants, around 2000 kind of medicinal plants including *Arogyapacha*, one of most used medicinal plant in Ayurvedic and siddha systems of treatment. It is one among the twenty new sites added by UNESCO to its World network of Biosphere Reserves in March 2016. This region turns to be an important tourist centre of attraction due to its geography, natural vegetation, wildlife and accessibility with new tourism department-sponsored programs. Kottoor Kappukadu Elephant Rehabilitation Centre, Neyyar Wild Life Sanctuary, Lion Safari Park, dams like Peppara and Neyyar, Palode Botanical garden, Ponmudi Hill station, Kallar Meenmutty waterfalls, Papanasam falls-the list continues. This region which covers 3500 sq km consists of numerous tourists pots can surely contribute a good income to the state.

The indigenous population found in this region is *Kanikkar*, also known as *Kanikaran*—one of the largest tribal population in Kerala. Kanikkar settlements are situated in the five states where

Agasthyar hills extend. Since it covers the border of Kerala and Tamil Nadu, this community is included in the scheduled list of both states. According to the myth of Agasthyar muni, Kanikkar consider him as the protector of their community. And the famous myth regarding the sage says that it is he who found the tribes in the forest and asked them to stop hunting and live in the forest to protect it resources. Some went to the sea shore and became mukkuva community or the fishermen, and some remained in the forest and they are these tribal community. Since the sage advised them for such kind of living, they worship him as a protector not deity. Later another reading of the same story can be seen in which he is compared to *parasurama* a legendary sage in Hindu mythology. Dr. M.V. Vishnu Namboodiri in his studies speak about this counter narrative and say that it is actually an attempt to get power over the tribal rituals and practises and integrate them to the Hindu community. This is another area where further research can been done on appropriation of mythical stories.

The history regarding their ownership over this land of Agasthyar hills goes such that the forest region where the hill situated was gifted to them by the king of Travancore as a token of gratitude for saving his life from enemies. Archaeological evidences of this like *chembupattayam* (document written on copper plate) is still preserved in the State Archaeological departments. This is the first record on the right of Adivasis over this Agasthyar forest region where they have been living for decades. Adivasis who lived in settlements did not hold separate documents for the land they possessed and they were unaware of getting the legal rights over their house and land. This system of living still continues among the tribes, which makes them landless even in this modern era. For years, they have continued their way of living, rituals and customs in this region without realizing the changes that are going on in the outside world. Over these decades no any external interventions happened in the tribal area but when the government-initiated projects were introduced in this region for the upliftment of tribes, the external influences and interference began to disturb their settlement. This has made good and bad impact on this people. One hand the education, medical employment and better housing are provided by government and on the other hand, the government demand for the legalization of documents makes them uncomfortable to cope up with the new circumstances. For example, when government decided to build houses for this people they were asked to give legal documents which prove their right over the piece of the land now they are living on. This force the inhabitants to divide the entire settlement land into small segments. A kind of losing community culture is the result of these changing modes of land ownership.

Tourism, a recently flourished business, has realized the scope of ecotourism in this region and introduced many tourist friendly projects. "Agasthyakoodam Trek" is a part of this big project which invites a good number of tourists to this region of Agasthyar Hills. There already existed a pilgrimage in the Agasthya hills by several traditional practisers who has faith in tribal rituals. This custom of pilgrimage was replaced by the Agasthyakoodam Trek program. Almost a decade back tourism department-initiated trekking journey began, until that the traditional way of pilgrimage and worshipping of sage *Agasthyar muni* continued. A statute of *Agasthyar muni* was maintained on top of Agasthyar hills where the Kanikkar tribes perform their rituals. The pilgrimage was carried out as a part of this festival. When government introduced the trekking journey it was propagated as an adventurous trekking journey which has nothing to do with the previous ritual practices. It purely focused on the tourist attracting program. The year in which tourism department seized the pilgrimage is not clear but from sources it found can be found that online registration started by 2013. A bifurcation of trekking and pilgrimage was now established in this Reserved

Forest region. For registration a person need to pay thousand rupees and initially the number of people permitted was four to six per day which now has become hundred per day. According to official records the number of tourists permitted is thousand but the real number exceeds three thousand. Most of the visitors are from the state itself and only few are foreigners. Usually the trekking was arranged in the month of January-February and extended to two months, a period of exactly sixty days. Whereas the number of days permitted for Kanikkar to practise their rituals at the top of hills are three. This gives the clear picture how things move out of the hands of tribes. Moving to history, after 1880s most of the forest became Reserved Forest including Agasthya region, and the government declared protection for tribes to practice their rights along with restricting forest destruction. But it is found that, in 1984 the numbers of family evacuated for the construction of Peppara dam was 44. In 1992 for the construction Agasthyarkoodam Wildlife Sanctuary 51 tribal families were evacuated from the region later provided with concrete buildings which they neglected. Similarly a large number of replacements happened in the tribal settlements of Agasthyar region in the name of development.

As a part of projects like Responsible tourism or Sustainable tourism, government has raised tribal recruitment to the jobs associated with tourism, and thus most of the Kanikkar tribes of Agasthyar region are working as part time guides. They get employment during the trekking period which causes them to support tourism in this region without understanding the further environmental consequences. They were unaware about the increase in number of tourists in this area. Even though tourism department has the higher percentage of tribal employees, the representation of tribes in top grade job is less. Many of them are working in the government-sponsored guest houses as sweepers, cooks, helpers etc. Government has never initiated or discussed these kinds of policy changes with tribal people. The tribal employees are working under the hegemony of state policy makers. This is the way how they have captured a land owned and worshipped by tribes and later employed the very tribes. The whole process happen in different stages of taking away land from the tribes, making it into reserve forest in the name of protection and finally introducing tourism programs on the protected reservoirs. Development, tourism and income are justification that authorities give for this injustice of humiliation they do to the tribal people. Agasthyakoodam trekking and Kanikkar tribes are representative example for the issues faced by the entire tribal population with the intrusion of tourism into reserved forests. From *Koragar* to *Kanikkar* around 35 tribal communities live in the Western Ghats and have different kinds of customs, myth, and beliefs regarding their land. This was shattered by the establishment of univocal tourism policies. Especially the districts like Idukki and Wayanad are facing serious environmental and tribal settlement issues where the tourism works at its peak.

Tribes, who considered *Agasthyar muni* as their protector, worship him still and continue the rituals for the sake of their belief system and for protecting traditional medicinal practises. They regard it as a means by which the entire Agasthyar region, medicinal plants, wild life, forest resources which were once gifted by the saint can be preserved. The ritual and pilgrimage is to protect Agasthyar region from any kind of destruction. On the other hand we have the tourism program that formed parallel to the pilgrimage which does a massive kind of destruction to this eco sensitive region. The objectives are very clear: one advocates for protection where another promote the tourism business for income. This is the way most ecotourism projects, wildlife sanctuaries and national parks work all over the developing nations. Aboriginals are one among those subjects that suffer due to the wildlife and tourism policies. Not only their system of belief is questioned, they were evacuated from their habitat along with their culture.

Now the Kanikkar community needs to get approval from the forest department to move to the hill top. The number of tribes can who can accompany is two hundred and the list should be given a week before to get approval. Very recently there occurred two agitations: one regarding the women's entry to Agasthyarkoodam which the tribes protested, but later they accepted the court order and withdrew from their movement. A second issue was regarding the removal of fence made around the statute of Agasthyar. Forest department has made the fence to protect the statute from tourists. Ironically the idea of protecting the entire region reduced to the idea of protecting the statute alone. Tribes who usually will not build fence or wall around their worshipping area demand for the removal of this fence, because every year pilgrimage ends with the "pretnishtapooja" (a ritual of worshipping Agasthyar statute). After the agitation only did the authorities promise to remove the fence temporally for three days' rituals. These are minor noticed conflicts which occurred in the tribal settlements when tourism encroached into the forest reservoirs.

To conclude, a tribal practised ritual for the protection of natural habitat gets commodified under tourism. Aboriginals who consider their myth and belief as sacred always try to keep their rituals away from outsiders. When government framed policies for tourism under the name of forest protection, opinions of tribes were not considered. Absence of their representation in this policy-making sectors, illiteracy, lack of knowledge regarding tourism and its changes in their settlements make the frazzle. Either this people move into other settlements or come out of the forest accepting low grade government jobs, both of which destructed the already existing "ooru culture" (community living culture). The establishment of tourism within the tribal worshipping region leads to vast destruction of environment; this is due to lack of knowledge regarding the purpose of their rituals. It is not possible to expect that the tourist will consider the region as the pilgrims does, hence environmental degradation is the cause. Addressing these issues is important, not just to protect tribal culture but an entire ecosystem rich with medicinal resources. Frequent visit of more than three thousands of tourists to the reservoir is more than enough to cause ecological imbalance to this forest region. The government-sponsored policies like this should be rechecked, hence, Agasthyarkoodam is not a unique case. There are so many similar sites in Kerala; which especially cover the Western Ghats, where pilgrimage turns tourism. Situation demands for sustainable tourism and its strict implementation along with aboriginal-involved policies.

Works Cited

Ajayan, K.R. *Agasthyakoodathile Adivasikal*. Thiruvananthapuram: Bhasha Institute. 2009.

_____. *Kanikadhakalude Rashtreeyam*. Thiruvananthapuram: Bhasha Institute, 2015.

"Agasthyakoodam Trek." Kerala Trip Guide. 7 February 2014. www.keralatripguide.com/thiruvananthapuram/agasthyakoodam-trek

Agasthakoodam Trek "Agasthya Mala" *Wikipedia: The Free Encyclopaedia*. https://en.wikipedia.org/wiki/Agastya_Mala

Gadgil, Madhav. "Environmentalism at the Crossroads." *Ecological Journeys: The Science and Politics of Conservation in India*. New Delhi: Permanent Black, 2001: 121-135.

Glotfelty, Cheryl. "Literary Studies in an age of Environmental Crisis." *The Ecocriticism Reader: Landmarks in Literary Ecology*, ed. Cheryl Glotfelty and Harold Fromm. Athens: U of Georgia Press, 1996: xx-xxv.

Gopinathan, R. "The Myth of Parasurama: The Issues on writing the socio-cultural History of Kerala." *Kerala Calling*. 25.12 (2005): 14-19.

Kala, B. *Chattupattum Samskaravum*. Nooranad: Unma P, 2009.

Karunakaran, C. K. *Aadivasikalude Lokam Vanavasikal*. Thiruvananthapuram: Bhasha Institute. 2007.

. . . *Kanikkar*. Thiruvananthapuram: Bhasha institute. 1989.

Namboodiri, M.V. Vishnu. "The Ancient Myth of the Aborigines." *Kerala Calling*. 24.9(2004): 31-34.

Sabastian, M. *Kanikkarude Lokam*. Thiruvananthapuram: Adikala Ezhuthukazhcha, 1990.

Sasikumar, K and R. Binu. "Neyyar: An Eco Paradise," *Kerala Calling*, 27.2 (2006): 40-41.

Thurston, Edgar and K. Rangachari. "Kanikkar" *Caste and Tribes of Southern India*. Delhi: Low Price Publications. 1909. 162-77

Mapping the Touchstones of Indigenous, Tribal and Subaltern Literatures in English

NAGESHWAR RAO KONDA

"We resist, we protest, we question and we survive." Ignited with the axiom, the 20th century witnessed the quest for the movements of identity and self respect. Indigenous literature is a story or piece of writing expressed by people who are indigenous to the country. They often express their traditions, relationships, suppression and sufferings. They may be in the form of poetry, plays and novels and so on. In fact many indigenous cultures in the world are deeply associated with the oral tradition like folklore, myths, ballads, stories; usually the indigenous people go through marginalization, subaltern consciousness identity and self respect. It is observed that around 400 million indigenous people follow unique traditions based on their socio-cultural and geographical means. The UNO and the ILO have outlined some of the characteristics of indigenous group based on their invasion, marginalization, cultural and economic practices etc.

Tribal literature is a new force which has emerged to channelize the cultural trajectories of tribes due to exploitation and identity. It is noted that the last decade of the 20th century showed the path to the galaxy of social movements like women, farmers, dalits and tribals and the oppressed for their upsurge in the democratic space. They have strongly stood against the exploitation and supremacy. In addition to socio-political movements, literary and cultural awakening and they have stood against the inequality and the exploitation of the downtrodden.

The tribal literature and its various forms were cut off from the mainstream literature because the literary tradition of the tribals was mainly oral and they were ignored by the canonic literature. On the other hand, in the light of liberalization policies, lakhs of tribals have been displaced in many states of India and the same situation has existed in many countries. In this connection the United Nations observed the year 1993 as the "International year of the Indigenous People." After this declaration, there was a long debate over the status of the tribals in India, since they were subjected to social, political and economic discrimination. If it is so, what type of discrimination? These questions and consequences manifested in the art, culture and literature. Each phase generating newer genres and styles influenced the mainstream writing.

Literature is always a reflection of the life around us. Literature looks into many factors both internal and external that have gone into the creation of that place and society. In order to understand the essence of the indigenous literature, there is a need to understand the background behind these movements. In fact indigenous literature is the literature of a search for identity, the various forms of exploitation and the challenges faced by the indigenous people. In the early days of the journey of the tribal literature, it was confined to consolidation, sympathy and empathy.

In the American context, Native American literature was significant. The early works highlighted the history, culture and growth of the America. Folk tales have been a part of the social and cultural life of Native American literature.

In the Indian context, tribal literary tradition has become a discourse. It opens the discussion on several issues connected to the indigenous culture, tribal society, history, language, traditions and practices. Some of the magazines played a significant role in moulding the shape of the tribal literature. They are Yuddhrat Aam Admi (Hazaribagh, Delhi), Aravali Udgosh

(Udaipur), Adivasi Satta (Chhattisgarh) etc. Gradually regional magazines and literary journals have provided the space to the tribal writings. Subaltern literature in Telugu, as in other Indian languages, passed through many phases. They try to put the question at each point by asking the root causes for their suppression.

Multiculturalism is the most important idea that no system of values is superior to any other; it emerged in the last part of the 20th century as answer to the genuine demands from various ethnic minorities. Especially in America, multiculturalism has inspired the various aspects of American life including media, socio-economic institutions, arts and literature. Diana Ravztch, who advocates a moderate approach, says: "Today pluralistic multiculturalism must contend with a new, particularistic multiculturalism. The pluralistics seek a richer common culture, the particularists insist that no common culture is possible or desirable."

In the world of today, there is an urgent need to talk about the indigenous and tribal languages and their implications and in the varieties of literature written in English and English translation, especially by the indigenous people who have settled down in their native land and explored newer vistas of the creative exploration. It is noteworthy to share the intellectual responsibility of scholars towards the socio-political and cultural things of the country. As Emerson said: "The book, the college, the school of art, the institution of any kind, stop with some past utterance of genius. . . . But genius looks forward; the eyes of man are set in his forehead, not in his head; man hopes; genius creates" (*American Scholar*, section II).

As Emerson said, "Man thinking" must look into the literary evidence for inspiration in creating his own thoughts. When human being creates his/her own thoughts, using every literary reflection to help him in his/her thought, only then will the scholar be truly learned. Thus it is evident that indigenous literature has to be exposed in order to highlight it in the contemporary literary arena.

Tradition or the total content of an indigenous heritage is kept alive through study, appreciation and healthy criticism and it is enabled through contact with other traditions and new ideas to refresh itself and march towards the future (Iyengar 584). In an outspoken article on the 'Indian Intellectual,' Nirad C. Chaudhari remarked: "Today, in our country, virtuality no intellectual effort is perceptible, if by intellectual effort is meant a ceaseless activity of self-criticism, both personal and national, and the steady formulation of new ideas, values and ideals. That kind of intellectual activity seems to have gone out of contemporary fate" (Iyengar 585)

African American literature has focused on the role of people of African descent vis-à-vis the larger American society what it means to be American. It is appropriate to quote a few lines from the poem titled "stage" penned by the Dalit poet, Waharu Sonavane:

> We did not go on to the stage
> Neither were we called.
> We were shown our places,
> Told to sit.
> But they, sitting on the stage
> Went on telling us of sorrows,
> Our sorrows remained ours,
> They never became theirs" (Negotiating Margins 17)

The above lives speak about the marginalization and subaltern expression and also show the real factors for their anxiety and suffering since ages.

It is worthy to mention Toni Morrison who writes about the life of black people in contemporary America. She presents the anxieties and aspirations, strengths and short comings of the blacks. Her fictional world is inhabited by people influenced by racist and sexist values. The marginals were so marginalized that coming to the centre was a scaring prospect for them. (Das 21)

Indian is known for its diversity. Diversity is present in religion, language, culture, art and so on. In fact the government of India has recognized twenty one official languages and about 900 languages spoken in the country. But the tribal literature has not been recognized as the mainstream literature. However it is the prime responsibility of the lovers of literature, social activists and the academicians to encourage the conversation and translation of these unheard voices and to share the literary germs with the outer world. Some of the scholars and academicians have come forward by translating the rare literary pieces into English. They have offered a fresh perspective to the global audience and made an attempt of conserving rare literature through translation.

In the postcolonial context, the concept of indigenous and subaltern literature generated by the theories and ideologies has to be escalated. The various discourses like caste, race, gender, marginality have mushroomed in the light of the modern outlook and they have to be made as the part of the mainstream literature. It is the need of the hour to rethink them in the specific dialectical, cultural and multi lingual context.

Works Cited

Nibir K. Ghosh and E. Ethelbert Miller, ed., *Charles Johnson: Embracing the World*, Authors Press, New Delhi 2012

N.M. Aston, ed., *Literature of Marginality: Dalit Literature and African-American Literature*, Prestige, 2001

Rodriguez, Valerian ed. (2002), *The Essential Writings of B.R. Ambedkar*, Oxford University Press, New Delhi

A. Karunaker, ed., *Negotiating Margins: African American and Dalit Writings,* Prestige Books International, New Delhi, 2013

K.R. Srinivasa Iyengar, *Indian Writing in English*, Sterling, New Delhi, 2013.

http://www.wikipedia.org/indigenous literature

http://www.Tribal Literatures in India and the World

http://www.study.com/academy/lesson/American scholar by Emerson

Shruhi Das, *From Margin to the Center*, Manglam, New Delhi, 2007

K. Purushotham, "Black Lilies, Telugu Dalit Poetry", *Critical Quest*, 2013.

Tracing the Untouchables: A Study of Socio-Cultural Life of Dusadhs

RITU CHOURASIYA

The folk literature consists of stories, ballads, songs, proverbs, riddles etc. is essentially an oral literature, and all over the world, folk stories are transmitted by word of mouth from one generation to another generation. The term folklore was coined in 1846 by W.J. Thomas (1803-85), but the founder of the scientific study of the subject is commonly held by Jacob Grim (1785-1863). However, folklore has been approached in a different manner by various scholars. Max Muller (1823-1900) inferred it as evidence of nature myths, J.G. Frazer (1854-1941) states that the comparative study of primitive and popular folklore are mutually interdependent and explanatory; Malinowski and Radclife-Brown dealt folklore as important and integral element in a living culture.[1]

The nature of folk literature constitutes usually fairy, ghost stories or stories related to animal and God with implausible background but intensely human and often emotional and always end with moral lessons. The folklores are not only for enjoyment or teachings but also give an insight of particular culture and tradition. Folktales are also useful source materials for artists to take insights for their artistic creation.[2]

As it has been already known that there are numerous languages and dialects present in every part of India and each language and dialect has infinite number of stories, poems, songs, riddles and proverbs. In case of Bihar, Bihari language consists of *Maithili*, *Magadhi* and *Bhojpuri*. There are many folk literatures present in Bihari languages. However, there are many folk-songs, stories and proverbs which are not present in written form, especially the folk stories of lower caste communities.

In this paper we are going to examine the folk stories and proverbs related to Dusadh community of Bihar. Dusadhs are Hindu lower caste community of Bihar who are also spread across the various regions of the country like Uttar Pradesh, Bengal, Orissa and Rajasthan. While tracing Dusadhs we found scanty written sources. Oral narratives held an immense importance while tracing them.

Dusadhs trace their origin from ancient time; the word 'Dusadh' is obsolete, this word is mentioned in Sanskrit mantra, which is translated by H.H. Wilson:

> Slay everyone who offers not libation, however difficult to be destroyed,
> Slay everyone who is not delight to you,
> Bestow upon his wealth, for pious (worshiper) deserves it.[3]

By this mantra Dusadh community is interpreted as ancient warriors, they are native and these native people are called 'Dusadhya' and they were protector of motherland.[4]

There is another folk story regarding the origin of Dusadhs which is present in Bhojpur region of Bihar which is narrated by Chhavinath Paswan and Manoj Yadav[5] which is not present in written form, as they narrates the story: "There were four women who did not have children, they all were very good friends and they used to go to Ganga river for worship. One day a saint came and gave one mango to one of them, that lady wants to consume the fruit alone, but then another lady saw and asked her why you want to consume this fruit alone then she told her that if she will eat this fruit she will give birth to a child, then other lady asked him to share the fruit with her, then she gave half piece of the fruit to the second lady, when second lady was returning to her home then she met third lady and the third lady asked about the fruit then she told the benefit of consuming food then third lady asked her to share fruit with her, when third lady was going to her home, on the way she met fourth lady then she told her the mystery of fruit then the fourth lady also asked her to share the fruit, in this manner the fruit has been shared by all four ladies, and after that they all gave birth to male child, and they all four belongs to four communities, *Dusadh, Dhobi, Yadav, Chamar* named *Dadhiya, Rajaii* and *Bachhava* respectively."

In this manner, they told me the famous narrative which is present in Bhojpur region of Bihar about the origin of these four castes including Dusadhs.

Coming to the occupation of Dusadhs, in an interview with Chhavinath Paswan,[6] he informs that the community is engaged in occupation of watchmen (*Chaukidari*), Henchmen (*lathaiti*), the Dusadhs women were engaged in household work, agricultural work and sometimes they assist their husband whatever he chose his profession. The men and women of Mithila region are engaged in occupation of Painting. *Madhubani Painting.*[7] In the book *Dusadh Jati: Udbhav aur Vikas* (2014) written by Vijay Kumar Trisharan, the information is similar to what it has been narrated by Chhavinath Paswan, it has been written that during medieval period the community is engaged in occupation of watchmen and in this region they are called '*Paswa*' (Pahredar) and they use 'Paswan' as their title. During the battle of Plassey, the community worked as troops and in colonial times the word 'Dusadh' has been used to denote *Pahredar* (Watchmen) of the village.

There are many folk stories related to Dusadhs among them few are available in written form in Hindi and Maithili and many stories are still unwritten. There are stories of King Sahlesh, Reshma and Chauharmal, and many folk plays (*Loknatya*) which depicts culture, and religious beliefs of the community.

The story of king Sahlesh and Dauna Malin has rarely been described in mainstream literature. Sahlesh is regarded as hero of

Dusadh community, he is also considered as son of Rahu.[8] There is no written evidence of Raja Sahlesh. Different folk plays and folk songs have considered Sahlesh as warrior and mighty king who always took care of his subjects. G.A. Grierson has translated some songs sung by ladies, referring to Sahlesh as lord or lover.

Dauna expresses her desire and love for king Sahlesh, she folds her hands and prays to fifty-six crores god and goddesses that she wants to meet Sahlesh and said that she is loyal to Sahlesh; she has not eyed upon any another man.[9] She has also mentioned about her pain and sorrow that if she will not meet Sahlesh she will die, she left her house but she didn't find any traveler that can take her message to Sahlesh.[10] This story is also narrated by Shivan Paswan of Madhubani region it is documented in a documentary named 'Folklore of Raja Sahlesh.'[11]

There is another Folksong related to Sahlesh in which his wife Satyvati is expressing her painful condition without Sahlesh:

> Ge Sun-Sun Bahina
> Tora Kahechhe dil ke batiya,
> Kekra kehbaik ke patiyotek
> Ge jekra kehbaik
> Saih latiyotaik ge
> Ge Aagik laheriya ham pani se bujhaibe ge
> Mana ke lehriya kona kai bujebe ge, ge didi sab.[11]

In above lines the wife of Sahlesh expresses her pain for her sister: I am telling you my heart's voice, with whom I will share my things, I cannot tell my heart's desire to anyone, I have solution for the fire which can be quenched by water, but there is no solution for the rage inside me.

There is another famous story about Reshma and Chauharmal (also called Baba Chuhadmal) in local language. He was a brave man from Dusadh community who fought against the feudal system.[12] Chuhadmal belongs to non-Aryan community (Dusadh) and Reshma belongs to Bhumihar community. Reshma fell in love with Chauharmal but Chauharmal didn't want any association with her, in anger she tore her clothes and told her father that Chauharmal was responsible for her condition. As a result her brother and father attacked Chauharmal. In this fight, Reshma's father was killed by Chauharmal who fought bravely.[13]

However, Chauharmal is depicted as thief and dacoit in Mithila region of Bihar. There is a famous story about enmity between Sahlesh and Chauharmal. During the reign of Bhim Sain, Chauharmal challenged Sahlesh that despite his Chaukidari he has committed theft at Bhim Sain's fort.[14]

The Dusadh community is perceived as mannerless low tribe. The upper castes and British felt that the Dusadhs indulged in burglary and theft. In South Bihar *Chakai Dusadhs* are described as criminals.[15] There are communities like Magahiya doms and Paliwar Dusadhs who commit theft and are known for highway robbery and murdering people but that does not mean that they are always lured by wealth. They murder upper caste people because of anger against them. Many police officials were killed in colonial times because they branded the community as criminal. There are many proverbs related to lower castes and Dusadhs which show the mentality of upper castes towards them: 'Dusadh Jati Khaye neeche takke uche.'[16] The proverb meant that when Dusadh eats he is not focused towards his plate; his focus is here and there so that he can take anything from the house.

'Neech na chhode neechai, Neem na Chhode teetai.' The proverb is in context of lower communities of society that lower communities never leave low or sinful work just like *neem* never leaves its bitterness.[17]

'Chhoti jat kare utpat.' The proverb says that lower castes always destroy and disturb the things.[18]

The history of lower caste communities has never become part of main history writing, the folk literature related to these communities were never part of main literature. There could be different reasons behind this—first the Dusadhs has always been marginalized and neglected community, and most of the writers belong to upper castes, so, if we find any mention of Dusadhs in history books or literatures that is worldview of upper castes regarding them. Secondly, there are many folk songs, plays which depict different cultures of Bihar and how it is source of entertainment and education for the people which is preserved in oral narratives. There is scanty of written sources on Dusadhs and if few have written form that has not been translated in English thus, it's totally unknown to large number of readers. Thirdly, the documents, folk literatures, artifacts related to Dusadhs have got rare space in Indian archives and National museum or Bihar archives and state museum. Fourthly, few literatures written on Dusadhs are termed as 'Footpath literature' because the authenticity of publisher and sources has been always doubted. We cannot deny that there is exaggeration about Dusadhs in local books, the community has been linked with Gehlot dynasty and their glorious past has been highlighted. But we cannot totally deny these literatures because they give essence of local culture and what we often find out that the book published with big publisher has criss-cross information inscribed like 'so called Footpath literature'; they are mutually dependent on each other.

There should be more curiosity towards the meaning and methods of the folksongs, folk plays, and folk dances within the community rather than finding the so-called truth. The folk literature related to lower caste communities should be encouraged and an attempt should be made to bring it to main literature, as they depict culture of village farms and village courtyard and contribution of women in survival of these literatures. There should be literature which should be written on Dusadh perspective so, that we would be able to know their worldview regarding the society.

NOTES

1. Choudhury, 1968:5, 'Most of the scholars have recognized the link between heritage and folklore.'
2. *Ibid.* 'folktales have their wings they quickly migrate from one region to another and disseminate.'
3. Trisharan, 2014:75
4. *Ibid.* 'Dusadhs have fought with Aryans to protect their motherland, because of this Aryans has asked I*ndra* to protect them, and asked that the wealth of Dusadhs should be snatched and should be given to Brahmans.'
5. Yadav: Manoj Yadav is member of ahir community of Bihar who has provided information regarding folk tales related to different communities like *Chamar, Ahir*, *Dom* and *Dusadhs*. The interview was held on 8 February at Dumraon (Bhojpur region) of Bihar.
6. Paswan: Chhavinath Paswan—A member of Dusadh Community who worked in post office. The interview held on 9th February, 2017 at Dumraon (Bhojpur region) of Bihar.
7. Madhubani Painting is local art form of Bihar region which is painted by almost all communities of the state, but majorly it is painted by Brahmins, Kshatriya and among lower caste Dusadh community.'
8. Rahu and Ketu are worshipped as God among Dusadhs.
9. Jha,1979:60-61, 'She expresses her love in the way that she has put vermillion for him, she has made beautiful bridal chamber with fresh bamboos, she has decorated bed with crimson color, she will apply silver spots to her brow for sahlesh.'
10. *Ibid.* 'In conversation with her sisters, Dauna is saying that we all should go to Kamla river, where Sahlesh came to water his elephants, if we will find him there, we will lure him and take him to garden by magic and there they will make bridal chamber and Dauna and sahlesh will marry to each other.'
11. Kumar: Shivan Paswan part 1 & 2,

12. Jha and Kumar Jha,2005:221, "There are many mangal geets which are usually sung by ladies; there are few general songs which are sung by every community, they start any function by remembering their folk deity which says: *Awo Purab me Sumiran Kareechhe, Ugal deena nath ke, aa pachhim me sumiran karechhe, Meera Sultan k awoo, Uttar me Sumiran karechhee, Pancho Pandava Bheem kay, Jekar naiya chalay chhee sansar me, Dakhin me Sumiran Kareechee, Ganga Mai ke ja kar jalas, sheetal ho pran*' which means that each direction is dedicated to a particular god like Sun, Meera, Pandavas, Ganges in East, West, North and South respectively."
13. Trisharan, 2014:126
14. *Ibid*, p.133,
15. Jha, 1979:62
16. Daly 1916:73
17. Trisharan, 2014:166
18. *Ibid*:167
19. *Ibid*.

Works Cited

Daly, F.C. *Manuals of Criminal Classes Operating in Bengal*, The Bengal Secretariat place, Calcutta, 1916.

Grierson, G.A. 'Some Bhojpuri Folksongs,' *The Journal of Royal Asiatic Society of Great Britain and Ireland*, Vol. 18, No. 2 (April 1886), pp. 207-67.

Folklore of Raja Salhesh, by Shivan Paswan, (Part 1 & 2), Director Sunil Kumar, Art News Network, 11 October, 2011, Paswan Madhubani, Bihar.

Sunil Kumar, *Folklores of Raja Salhesh* (Theatrics of Raja Salhesh, Bihar) Sahapedia, April 7, 2018.

Chhavinath, (Dusadh Community), interview on 8 and 9 February, 2017, Dumraon (Bhojpur region) of Bihar.

Manoj Yadav, (Ahir Community), interview on 8 February, 2017, Dumraon (Bhojpur region) of Bihar

Shivmuni Thakur, (Nai Community), interview on 26 June, 2018, Chhotka Dhakaich (Bhojpur region) of Bihar

Diwakar R.R., *Bihar through Ages*. K.P. Jayswal Institute, Patna, 1959

Jha, Devkant and Dinesh Kumar Jha, *Maithili Natak Vikas,* Sahitya Akademi, New Delhi, 2005

Choudhury, Roy, P.C. *Folktales of Bihar*. Sahitya Akademi, New Delhi, 1968

Chaudhury, Kumar, Prasanna, *Svarg Par Dhava: Bihar me Dalit Aandolan*, 1912-2000,' Vani Prakashan, New Delhi, 2005

Jha Bhimnath, 'Maithili: A Fruitful Year,' *Indian Literature*, (Nov-Dec. 1980) Vol. 23, No. 6, pp. 43-54

Jha Makhan, *Folklore, Magic and Legends of Mithila,* Jyoti Classical, 1979

Orissini, Francessa, '*Print and Pleasure: Popular literature and entertaining Fictions in Colonial North India,'* Permanent Black, 2009

Trisharan, Vijay Kumar, *Dusadh Jati: Udbhav aur Vikas*, Samyak Prakashan, New Delhi, 2014

Native American Struggle: A Study of James Welch's *Winter in the Blood* and Sherman Alexie's *Reservation Blues*

P. SHOBHA

In the Montana that Welch depicts in his novel and poems, Indians drift in and out of white towns and bars, estranged from their traditional culture and security and meaning it afforded them. Welch is saying that history ended for the Indians when their traditional way of life ended, and days that were once filled with meaning for them are now meaningless. (Velie 79)

Native American is the term referred to American Indians living within the United States. During the World War II thousands of American Indians were serving in the U.S. military abroad and they were exposed to the mainstream of society life with poverty-ridden reservations. They were less accepted after the war, latter on the government of U.S. has assimilated policies to bring Indian people to main streams, it provided them with education opportunities and the population began to move in cities. The change of attitude in Americans made majority of American Indians to live in urban areas and their native pride and political identity remained the same among reservations.

The struggle and heritage of the authors related to Native American Renaissance was brought under limelight which included music, painting, sculpture and other arts and cultural expression in all these fields have revived and expanded in rest of U.S. to the presence of richly diverse with the presence of native cultures. The best example for other native writers is James Welch who had distinct voice and ever changing approach that has inspired his colleagues and fellow author Ivan Doig. Welch has written about Indians in Modern American society with clear voice from intimate perspective.

James Welch was born on 1940 in Browning, Montana, and was raised on the Blackfoot and Fort Belknap reservations. Welch's father was Black feet and his mother Gros Ventre, each having Irish ancestors. The World War II becomes the reason for the family to live in Portland, South Dakota, and Minneapolis and so on just due to reservation. He received his degree from the University of Montana and had also finished his study in creative writing in the university of MFA program. The first novel by Welch was *Winter in the Blood* (1974) which was also adapted as an independent film with same name which was produced by Native American writer Sherman Alexie. He is also best known for his novel *Fools Crow* (1986).

The works of Welch explore the experience of Native Americans from 19th and 20th centuries. He has also written poems and is an award-winning novelist who wrote with great power and sensitivity, and his fiction focused on two topics firstly on contemporary Indian life and other on historical material. Each novel of Welch explores new ways of storytelling which has authentic picture of real Native Americans. Along with novel the poetry of Welch features the American West, the first book of poetry, *Riding the Earthboy Forty*. The poem has good vision, history and people who experience with the depth of nativity sufferings which is focused with true theme and sorrowful expressions:

> It was always 'they' who found him, yet I had a memory as timeless as the blowing snow that we had found him ourselves, that we had gone searching for him after the third day, or fourth day, or the fifth, cruising the white level of highway raised between the blue-white. (13)

The first novel of James Welch is *Winter in the Blood* which is considered as depressing for white readers, as it represents the life in Northern Plain region. The novel represents a protagonist with no name, and he undergoes an identity crisis. The story reflects the life of young Indian who lives in Montana similar to the writer Welch as the protagonist also belongs to Blackfoot and also part of Gros Ventre Indian. The tribe to which protagonist belongs is poor and his culture is clashing with the white settlement of federal government.

The nameless protagonist suffers from family tragedies as his father died in a snowdrift and his brother at the age of fourteen was victim of fatal accident and his grandmother is also no more. His life is filled with anger, pain and humor which are part of his terrible journey; it is tentative to be from one misadventure to another. The man is not aware of his situation and he doesn't have any identity and finds himself in the situation of failure always.

The unnamed thirty-two year old man suffers from depression and he doesn't know the way to escape; he works as a farmhand of his step-father's property and keeps on questioning his strong-willed mother about past situations. He does not feel happy spending time in bars and small streets and towns of Montana. He fulfils his desires with white women and lives his life in a boring lonely way. The emotional incident in his life takes place when he is unable to rescue a cow suffocating death in a mudhole. The protagonist seeks for the counsel from Yellow Calf, who is an old blind Indian. He tries to grasp the truth of his past and present related to his origin and how it has deeply influenced his life.

The struggle of the characters with cultural and economic displacement and their desire to have purpose, for connections between the past and present circumstance to give meaning for the life they are leading is necessary to understand. This novel provides us hope to understand the lives of contemporary Native

Americans and their situations which seek them to find solutions and take the responsibility and see into the complexities of guilty and regret. In the beginning of the novel the protagonist doesn't recollect his past but by the end of the novel he tries to join the fragmented pieces of his cultural history, to confront his family history as this is the only way to overcome barriers to escape from the situation of alienation and proceed towards future with hope.

Sherman Alexie was born on 1966 and now lives in Seattle, Washington; he grows up on Spokane Indian Reservation. The writing of his experience comes from Indigenous American with ancestry from several tribes. Alexie wanted to receive better education so he attends white high school. He stays in Gonzaga University at the age of 18 and was later on transferred to Washington State University. Alexie wanted to become a doctor, but when he attended the classes of poetry taught by Alex Kuo, he started writing poetry and submitted it for magazine. The addiction for alcohol was too heavy for him but still he managed writing poetry. When his works started publishing he quit drinking and concentrated on writing books.

The best known book of Alexie is *The Lone Ranger and Tonto Fistfight in Heaven* (1993), which is a collection of short stories which was adapted into film as *Smoke Signals* and he was the one who wrote screenplay for it. *Reservation Blues* (1995) is the first young adult novel by Sherman which won National Book Award for Young People's Literature. The Native Americans who had to hand over their belief, religion and way of life after the coming of White Men. Native Americans were divided into many tribes before White Men entered their life. They use to preach their own religion and live life according to their own culture and tradition. The White Men won battle against them and acquired rule over them and started controlling their life.

The characters in *Reservation Blues* struggle with their identity. The story is about a group of Native Americans in Washington, who decide to form a blues band which they name as "Coyote Springs." The group has rise and fall; it includes the struggle of each individual member of the band because they belong to Native American life. The character named Victor has tied himself with the past and has trouble coping with life so he tries to battle constantly with in self and his surroundings.

An African-American model Robert Johnson is introduced in the opening scene. Johnson leaves behind his guitar which is considered as magical by Thomas. In the beginning the band plays in the local bars and receives fame so they travel to Seattle and New York. Later, they are forced to renounce pieces of their culture in the white society. Alexie wants his characters to accept the challenges of cultural interchange and face the experience of every aspect of life.

The Native Americans not only suffer with the identical issues but they also struggle with the New coming age of culture, still they have the spiritual power to overcome the whites and accept the changes according to time. These people are unable to overcome from poverty and culture of alcoholism and depression. The Native Americans are trying to maintain their cultural identity in dominated white world.

Horses play an important role in *Reservations Blues* as it indicates they were Indian horses which were considered as part of resemblance of hardworking people; it also represents different generation related to music. Alexie has highlighted the realities of Native Americans by introducing the characters who suffer from racial issues, intercultural problems, poverty and alcoholism. Alexie and Welch have common issues in their selected novels and the characters try to get fit into situation given to them with all the obstacles in life.

Works Cited

Alexie, Sherman. *Reservation Blues*. New York: Warner Books, 1995.

Hafen, P. Jane. "Rock and Roll, Redskins and Blues in Sherman Alexie's Work" *Studies in American Indian Literature* 9.4 (Winter 1997): 71-8.

Velie, Alan R. *Four American Indian Literary Masters: N. Scott Momaday, James Welch, Leslie Marmon Sitko and Gerald Vizenor*. Norman: University of Oklahoma Press, 1982.

Welch, James. *Winter in the Blood*. New York: Penguin Books, 1974.

Exposition on Canadian Feminism: A Comparative Study of Margaret Atwood's *The Edible Woman* and Margaret Laurence's *The Diviners*

V. JYOTHI

Margaret Atwood and Margaret Laurence, the two Canadian women writers, have great record of success as feminist writers and declared as "major" contemporary women novelists. The women's movement has made many women writers to break out of traditional forms to show how women have been abused, exploited, and oppressed. The two authors depict stories about female experience and explore condition of being female. There's much common in the private fears, loneliness, insecurity and dislocations. Atwood's writing is involved with human rights of women, the relationship between man and women and her feminist ideology has "a larger, non-exclusive picture" and she wrote "not as a writer, (but) as a human being." Her novels are determined by feminist consciousness which runs as under current and serves as unifying principle.

Atwood's *The Edible Woman* is the first Canadian novel, as the novel predates the Women's Liberation Movement. Atwood rightly describes *The Edible Woman* as "protofeminist" novel, it is constructed like a journey, self-discovery, self-identity of a woman called Marian, her association with many male and female colleagues, role models and friends makes her realize different male strategies of exploitation and the causes of women's oppression. Her experience with them is mostly unpleasant. Eventually, she brings up enough courage to turn the tables against men like Peter and Duncan who are out to exploit and humiliate her. Therefore she refuses to be "edible woman" deceived in domesticity. She struggles to attain humanity and a human identity. This paper seeks to clarify the progression of Marian from meek, submissive woman to a strong individualistic and active feminist. It explores and evaluates the choices and options before Marian while highlighting her feminist consciousness. J. Brooks Bouson says: "Atwood deploys her female protagonist, Marian MacAlpin, to expose and subvert the ideological constructs that have long defined and confined women" (Prabhakar 38).

Feminism both as a concept and a movement has emerged as a reaction against the atrocities of patriarchy. Throughout history, and in all civilizations, the personality of women has been sought to be damaged and perverted and her very status as a human being 'interiorized' under the overwhelming male-domination. Feminism is a global as well as a revolutionary ideology. Canadian women writing in the post-1960s played a key role in setting and in many radical ideas of women's individuality and autonomy, power and politics. The aim of the Canadian women's fiction is to make women conscious of their position in the standard social structures. Their writings are concerned with the exploration and survival, cross boundaries, challenging cultural and psychological limits. Women writers have aimed at restructuring social and economic relations in the light of gender equality in Canadian society.

Even though feminist theory itself is not a unified political ideology, all kinds of feminism share certain commonalties in their political perspective; each type of feminism offers a different perspective in the nature of women's oppression. Each of them has its roots in a long history and each needs to be understood in relation to mainstream. Liberal feminist theory is to gain equal rights for men and women. Modern societies must reform by revolutionary means. Radical feminist is of the view that patriarchy is the most basic of all social institutions. Society is divided into sex classes. All women are potential allies in the struggle against men and the patriarchal institutions supported by men. Socialist feminist tries to integrate socialism and feminism; it means feminist goals can only be achieved within a socialist society and the struggle against capitalism and socialism is equally important. Marxist feminism is sometimes also referred to as materialist feminism because of its emphasis on concrete, structural aspects of social organization; it distinguishes gender inequalities as deriving capitalism, class and economic exploitation.

It is interesting to know that there is a fundamental difference between Canadian and American literature. In American literature, the protagonists are compelled to split their roots and ties in order to come into their own identity and sense of self. Canadian literature does not support to the idea that leaving home is necessarily a cause for growth and development; very frequently Canadian protagonists return to their roots, seek to understand their past and the generations who come before them, in order to know who they really are. Returning their home is not seen as a defeat in Canadian literature, but in American literature they consider it as a defeat.

Morag in *The Diviners* makes a pilgrimage to Scotland by thinking it is her native land, but realizes her true home is in the Canadian Prairie and finds a release into an inner freedom and resolves her dilemma of identity and survival. Laurence empowers the marginalized voice: from Canada as contrast to US, and from prairie as opposed to a metropolis such as Toronto. Morag's husband Brooke Skelton identifies with the canonical standards of the British academic world. Morag's step parents offer her a disadvantaged background and in each case marginalized voice is elevated by a focus on gender.

Motherhood is a unique female experience and post feminist writings portray women proclaiming their womanhood and motherhood in a bold manner, glorifying their womanhood through their motherhood and homemaking. Clara is symbol of traditional motherhood who sacrificed everything to have her children and she is contrast to Ainsley's radical approach to motherhood. Morag's motherhood marks a new phase in her life. The sterility of Morag relationship with Brooke's marriage is not only represented by their final divorce but also by the enforced absence of children, but Morag's feminism is active, she rejects her domineering husband, bears and raises a child without support and pursues the activity of writing despite heavy social structures that make this profession more difficult for women than for men.

The river is major symbol which unifies the novel and it is one of most important images in the novel; there is both acceptance and assertion of movement of time and energy through all the generations of mankind, the edge of water is very clear, beyond it keeps its life hidden. River depths express mysteries in time for individuals, generations and nations; novel ending suggests mysterious human experience and its unity in diversity. Marian tries to create a new image of her by creating the cake she would like to show her feelings and symbolically, the cake-women represents woman as an object for male consumption. This symbolic gesture is evocative of Marian's release from emotional cannibalism. She begins to eat the cake ending her withdrawal from food as soon as Peter leaves the place; she asserts that she cannot be manipulated by the people like Peter and Duncan. She wants to become neither a man nor a machine but women who search for a meaningful identity. This has become sign of symbolic empowerment of women.

Marian experiences identity crisis in her company because all top positions were occupied by men and women have no freedom there is discrimination against women because marriage and pregnancy are treated by them in employment; " pregnancy as an act of disloyalty to company"(21). Marian rejects the consumerist glances and Duncan's male-dominance. They all decide to remain single as an individual and assert themselves by choosing their autonomy and independence. This novel pleads for a radical change with regard to gender relations in the society. It gives message that women are not mere objects of beauty meant for erotic consumption of men.

Peter, her boyfriend, likes Marian as she never demands anything from him and he proposes her. His opinion about Marian is "conventionalized even stereotyped image of women who minus her chastity, recalls the mid-Victorian Ruskinian image of passive and dependent women" (Tandon 102). She feels that her identity and interests can never be safe in the event of her marriage with Peter. Marian understands the true character of Peter as an exploiter and also feels that she has let herself sold as some kind of a dispensable commodity. The sensitive Marian happens to grow a kind of nausea for unsavory attitude of Peter and she chooses to eat very rarely.

As a realistic novel, it shows female passivity in the traditional wife and mother roles and this leads threat to very survival of the self. So Marian did not want to fall in the trap of decorative life where both her identity and individuality are supposed to be mercilessly crushed. Marian's loss of individuality is indicated by the silencing of the inner self and her rejection of food is caused by her subconscious rejection of victim role. Marian's relationship with Duncan shatters her completely; she decides to stop eating until she finds a solution for all chaos. As she leaves the Duncan, he asks her: "where do you go?" (Atwood 258) This query declares the plight of women, who are exploited, abused, divorced abandoned and oppressed. Thus she is made a symbolic cannibalism.

The women protagonists in Manawaka are all humanized and their journey towards survival and inner freedom in the mechanized, violent world, it focuses on the obstacles of women. She examines the dilemma of the question for identity and attempts to discover in fictional terms and to consider with the women's problems; these are preoccupied with national identity and assert a distinctive quest for Canadian identity. She writes within human tradition and endorses a more balanced view of man-women relationship.

Morag Gunn a prominent writer feels herself in a disturbed and distressed state of mind due to sudden growth of her daughter Pique adolescence to an unspecified destination leaving just a note behind. This immediate crisis makes her aware of her inability to arrive at a definite identity of herself. Having been orphaned at the age of four, she was brought up by Christie Logan, the town's garbage man and his wife from an English family; because of her feeling of self-hate for her past makes Morag leave Manawaka, her sense of loneliness in a university atmosphere brings her into contact with professor. She wants to be good wife, but her husband Brooke denies her womanhood and feels that she has given Pique a bad moment as mother. She is very strong female character of the novel. The search for self-knowledge is very difficult for Morag because she doesn't have family or parents. Morag's isolation rises from the loss of her parents and the fact she is unable to accept Christie and Prin as her real parents, who are marginalized and interiorized beings disrespected and distanced by society, fail to provide Morag any sense of identity. Morag Gunn is an outsider in every sense of the term. As she grows older, Morag recognizes her position of alienation. This novel in particular is concerned with the archetypal human quest; the mother-daughter relationship is used as the very principle of structural and thematic organization.

Morag Gunn's journey towards self-discovery indeed becomes a journey of Canadian identity by merging together personal and national history so that it becomes not only Morag individual's story but a story of the nation. Morag experiences many barriers that can stand between a woman and creativity includes her husband's ego, morning sickness and sleeping children. Morag re-discovers her roots for an appropriate self-perception; the Canadian writers should similarly do the same to resolve the Canadian problematic of the quest for identity. Marian needs freedom to develop her personality and refuses to be an "edible woman." It is the sign of her feminine valour and her capacity for wholeness. The search for Canadian identity, discrimination encountered by women find place in the works of both authors. Their protagonists in the beginning of the novels might be victims but by the end of novel they refused to being victimized. Their state of desolation is changed into a state of wholeness by their journey and it becomes a journey towards self-hood and an acceptance of their heritage.

Works Cited

Gibson, Graeme. *Margaret Atwood, Eleven Canadian Novelists*. Toronto: Anansi, 1973, p. 25.

Howell, Coral Ann. *Modern Novelist: Margaret Atwood*. Hampshire London: Macmillan, 1996, p. 49.

Atwood, Margaret. *Survival: A Thematic Guide to Canadian Literature*. Toronto: House of Anansi Press, 1972, p. 209.

Atwood, Margaret. *The Edible Woman*. McClelland and Stewart. 1969.

Laurence, Margaret. *The Diviners*. Toronto: McClelland and Stewart. 1974.

Thomas, Clara. *The Manawaka World of Margaret Laurence*. Toronto: McClelland and Stewart. 1976.

John William, Keith. *An Independent Stance: essays on English Canadian Criticism and fiction*. The University of Toronto Press. 1934.

Salat, M.F. *The Canadian Novel: A Search for Identity*. D.K 1951.

Baily, Nancy. *Margaret Laurence, Carl Jung and the Manawaka Women: Studies in Canadian Literature*. 1977.

Buss, Helen. M. *Mother and Daughter Relationships in the Manawaka Novels of Margaret Laurence*. Victoria: University of Victoria Press. 1985.

Insights of Sexuality in Disabled Women

BOLLA MADHAVI

"I am attractive, witty, I want to be touched. I want to be loved romantically. I want to experience my sexuality, but I cannot because I am disabled," asserts Malini Chib in her famous interview: "I am single because of my body." (2012)

In 2011, Malini Chib, a disability rights activist and author who has cerebral palsy, wrote in an online article: "The word sex and disability don't go together. Can disabled people have sex? Tauba tauba! A topic best not mentioned. Even though I have been brought up in a westernized, liberated family and social strata—the topic has rarely been brought up with me. Most people think that if they start the conversation, they will hurt my feelings. Why does the topic sex frighten everyone when it comes to disabled people?"

"I have had a hard time accepting that I am trapped in a rejected body. A body that is not sexually attractive. . . . Like most women, sometimes I craved to be in the arms of a man. Most men look at me as asexual." These are the lines from Malini Chib's work *One Little Finger*. She concedes that she is looked down upon by the people as asexual, denoting many women with disabilities as of the same prejudiced notion. Malini Chib, a survivor of Cerebral Palsy, a famous disability activist from India, redefines her compromised body.

Renu Addlakha, a social scientist and disability rights researcher at the Centre for Women's Development Studies (CWDS) in New Delhi said, "Sexuality is an area of distress, exclusion and self-doubt for persons with disabilities." (Sexuality and Disability in the Indian Context, 18)

Shelley Nixon's *From Where I Sit*, tells her life with cerebral palsy, where she asserts, "my book is an autobiography, I am not unique. I don't want sympathy. I want to see people, who have CP, and other disabilities, and accept us as people." She also talks of being frustrated, when others judged her with her disability.

Body becomes the cage, a prison cell, for a woman with disability. Yet, she wishes to see herself to be loved. But, society gives marginal position to her. Women, when compared with men, are forced to experience double disadvantaged situations, often their rights are taken away, for example, rights to motherhood, rights to sexuality. Their bodies are treated as the sights of punishment for their sins of their previous birth, which is still continued in some rural areas. But, their bodies contain the usual desires of sexuality, love, acceptance. Sexual rights and reproductive rights of women with disabilities are less discussed topics in our society and even in our literature.

The World Health Organization (WHO) offers a working definition of sexuality that is broadly accepted: Sexuality is a central aspect of being human throughout life and encompasses sex, gender identities and roles, sexual orientation, eroticism, pleasure, intimacy and reproduction. Sexuality is experienced and expressed in thoughts, fantasies, desires, beliefs, attitudes, values, behaviors, practices, roles and relationships. While sexuality can include all of these dimensions, not all of them are always experienced or expressed. Sexuality is influenced by the interaction of biological, psychological, social, economic, political, cultural, ethical, legal, historical, religious and spiritual factors.(WHO, 2006a) (Sexuality and Disability in the Indian Context, 13)

Sexual education is pre requisite for women with disabilities. Women with disabilities sometimes, are not aware of the victimization that surrounds them, sometimes feared of expressing their abuse, and not confident that, weather their acquaintances will believe or not about their abusive experiences. Women with disabilities are constrained to express their sexual desires, and forced to repress their desires from childhood by the family and society.

"I have been abused by care givers, family, boyfriends, nurses and doctors, and even by other disabled people my entire life" Karen shares her experiences in a news paper interview.

Abuse becomes the terrific aspect of forced sexuality for women with disabilities. The irony is, their basic rights of sexuality are denied, and they are subjected to abusive, tortured, forced sexuality which in turn result in traumatic memories, unwillingness for sexuality. In decoding these processes of bodily images, the images of their bodies viewed by society, cultural constructions of marriage for women with disabilities.

Women with disabilities are sometimes not aware of the victimization that surrounds them, sometimes feared of expressing their abuse, and not confident that, whether their acquaintances will believe or not about their abusive experiences. Woman with disabilities are constrained to express their sexual desires, and forced to repress their desires from childhood by the family and society.

Even before adulthood girls are taught to admire and strive after prettiness. The fairy stories they read as children encourage this—the pretty Cinderella triumphs over her ugly sisters; Sleeping Beauty is an attractive woman whose beauty is enhanced by her passivity in sleep. Neither is usually portrayed as anything other than a Barbie doll-like creature with long, golden hair, slim waist and elegant limbs. In each case, their beauty is rewarded and their full flowering reached by marriage to a prince, just as the ugliness of Cinderella's two sisters is punished by the intimation of a lonely life of spinsterhood. The moral of both stories is clear: evil comes in the shape of ugly women, poverty and misshapen witches; good in the shape of pretty women, wealth, princes and physical perfection. (*Women and Disability* 64)

Disabled women have less sexual experiences; and if they have them, these are with trauma, and terror, limiting their pleasure of sexuality. They have space-related limitations, not having economic independence, having gender-based discrimination, are the obstacles for sexual life.

In India, disability is often seen as bad karma. As Renu Addlakha says: "Indeed the law of karma decreed that being disabled was the just retribution for past misdeeds. Pity, segregation, discrimination and stigmatization became normalized in the management of persons with disabilities. Such constructions of the disabled by the non-disabled have the dual effect of not only justifying the complete marginalization and disempowerment of a whole population group but also leading to the internalization of such negative stereotypes by disabled persons themselves." (Sexuality and Disability in the Indian Context 18)

Women with Disabilities are the most vulnerable group in our society. They experience this vulnerability because of their gender, disability and poverty. Disabled women face the humiliation more than Disabled men. In a patriarchal society usually birth of a son is always celebrated and the birth of the girl child treated as an unwelcomed child. And the birth of a disabled girl always considered as a sin of their previous birth.

In her remarkable essay "On Being a Cripple" Nancy Mairs concedes, "society is no readier to accept crippledness than to accept death", portraying the cruelty of the society where women with disabilities live in isolation. As she further claims: "what I hate is not me, but my disease" (Mairs).

Women with disabilities do like their bodies, but hate being seen as disabled or diseased. These women voice their hatred towards the charity organizations which colonize their sexuality for money, and exhibit the power relations where able men and women control the women with disabilities physically and psychologically.

We should talk about the importance of identifying the rights of fertility and sexuality for women with disabilities, which will create a more inclusive society. Society should come out from the stereotypical notion of assigning motherly, wifely roles for women, and giving them traditional, household works, as those stereotypical notions are labeling women with disabilities as asexual, incapable of performing household work, preventing them from marriage, child care, and other social activities. Still, girl child is treated as unwelcome in few families, and woman with disability are in a most disadvantaged situation where society prefers their death than their lives. Coupled with disabilities, their intellectuality, their achievements are simplified and reduced, when treated remarkable as they are disabled, and often called as inspirational. At this juncture, sexuality becomes another part of identifying the personhood of a woman with disability.

Acquiring disability for a married woman, prevents her healthy marital life, sometimes becomes a threat to sustain that marriage. But in contrast, disabled men, enjoy the same marital life, their marriage is rarely broken. This kind of difference exists between men with disabilities and women with disabilities, and stresses that disability is a social construct; if the disability can be ignored, an equal society can be achieved.

Works Cited

Sexuality and Disability in the Indian Context. Working Paper. TARSHI. 2018.

Lonsdale, Susan. *Women and Disability: The Experience of Physical Disability among Women*. 1990.

Chib, Malini. One Little Finger. Indian, 2012.

Nixon, Shelley. "From Where I Sit; Making my way with Cerebral Palsy," *Scholastic*, 1999.

Mairs, Nancy. "On Being a Cripple", *Disability Studies*. unc.edu.2016/01.

Sabarimala Untold: The Brahminisation of an Adivasi Deity

JOBINRAJ R.V & DHINIL SEN

The tribal community is one of the largest in the Indian subcontinent. They form a majority of the population in today's social structure. According to the Indian census of 2011, they form 8.6 per cent of the Indian population. The different tribes within India are not divided evenly. The highest density of scheduled tribes within India is constituted within Mizoram and the islands of Lakshadweep while the least is in Haryana and Punjab. There are a variety of tribes concentrated all over India, the most prominent being the Gonds, the Bhils and the Santhals among various others. The Scheduled Tribes are also called 'Adivasis' as an umbrella term within India. It is an amalgamation of the Sanskrit term 'adi' and 'vasi' meaning 'origin' and 'dwellers' respectively.

The various Adivasi tribes within India have their own language, rituals and practices. In some cases, they have a few similarities but in others, they are wildly different. Most of the tribes lived in peaceful harmony before the advent of the British Empire into India. The advent of the colonial rule brought forward various reforms that changed the structure of the entire tribal populace within India. Most of the tribal communities within India identify with a particular religion or practice within their demographics. These religions can be Islam, Hinduism or Christianity being the major influences within India. In keeping with the nature of the various Indian religions generally, these particular tribes often involve traditions or conventions of ancestor worship or worship of spirits of natural origin. There is often ambiguity on how most tribal practices take place. The tribal practices within each of the tribes vary depending on the religion it has its influences from. For example, Hinduism has influenced many tribes in India. Hinduism attributes sacred status to many animals such as the peacock, cobras and elephants and plants such as the sacred fig, the holy basil *(tulsi)* and the Indian lilac *(neem)* which may once have held symbolic importance for certain Adivasi tribes. Most of the tribes have their own customs and practices indigenous to them.

The tribal communities in Kerala, the southern state of India, have their own set of tribes and practices and are endemic to the Western Ghats, bordering Karnataka and Tamil Nadu. They are mostly forest dwellers and live as one with nature. Of the fourteen districts of Kerala, Wayanad has the highest density of tribal communities followed by Idukki and Palakkad. The tribal communities can be divided according to their level of awareness of the outside world. The tribes that are low on the scale of literacy rates can be termed 'primitive tribes.' The tribes of Cholanaikkans, Kurumbas, Kattunayakan, Kadars and Koragas are often included in this classification. They are evenly distributed from Northern Kerala's Malappuram and Kozhikode district, to Central Kerala's Thrissur and Palakkad, to the Southernmost district of Thiruvananthapuram. Most of the tribes within Kerala, speak a variety of Malayalam, with varying degrees of inclusion of the popular aspect of the language. Others adopt a variant which is mixed with either Kannada or Tamil or an amalgamation of the three main languages. Most of the new generation of tribal members do speak the native tongue of Kerala and are more susceptible to the way of the common people of the land. The customs and rituals followed by the tribes have some commonalities. They are very close to nature and worship it. However, this has seen a progressive decline in the light of imposition from outside influences. They also live with materials found in the forests, surrounding their abode. They do not venture outside their central zones (i.e. herein, their forest space) and although they accept outsiders and are not hostile, they are sceptical of strangers who dare to venture into their space.

The point of emphasis within this paper is upon the Mala Arayars belonging to the Central part of Kerala. They are, like other tribal communities, closer to the forest. Mala Araya, derived from the word "Malai Arayan" meaning "Monarch of the Hills", is one of the largest tribal communities in the areas of the Kottayam, Idukki and Pathanamthitta districts of Kerala. They are also called "Mala Arayans" or "Mala Araya." It must be noted that until recently the Uralis and Ulladans—other prominent tribes—addressed the Malai Arayan as 'Vazhiyan' for the men or 'Vazhathiyaramma,' for the female respectively. These terms attribute to the status once enjoyed by the Malai Arayans. An 'Arayan,' in the traditional sense meant 'one who is faithful to the religion of the clan.' Compared to other communities within Kerala during that point of time, the Mala Arayars enjoyed the comfort of wooden houses while their counterparts sufficed with mud houses. There were no beggars among the Malai Arayans. They hunted with the muzzleloader, a type arms into which the projectile and usually the propellant charge is loaded from the open end. The concept of magic fascinated them. They were also environmentally conscious. Rev. Samuel Mateer, a Christian missionary, from London who played a major role in the formation of the Church of South India (CSI) in Kerala and also established London Mission Society (LMS) in Kerala, points out that the caste Hindus placed the Mala Arayans on par with the Jewish diaspora in Kerala.

There are many folklores surrounding the origin of the Mala Araya community. Some Mala Arayars claim to be descendants from Rishi Gautama and Ahalya, after their troubled unification. Others claim that the Mala Arayars descend from Lord Siva and Sage Agastya. The legends follow that Lord Siva created a couple and Sage Agastya destroyed them but recreated them from fire. The community believes that they descended from the four children of this very couple. The four children, they believe, is what led to the distinctions; i.e. sub-groups within the Mala Arayars—the Mala Arayans (Lord of the Hills), the Ottaruyan (The Palanquin bearers of the Maharaja), the Katalarayan (Lord of the Sea), and The Nataruyan (The Maharaja) (Iyer 163). One of the most pressing matters to be noted within today's context is the link between the Mala Araya community and the erstwhile Ayyappan. It is said that Ayyappa was born within the tribal community to a couple, Kandan and Karuthamma, in Ponnambalamedu. According to K. P. Sajeev in an interview to The Caravan, an online journal of politics and culture, he mentions about the folklores of Kandan and Karuthamma and Ayyappan. He also mentions about the forty-one day fast.

During this period of history, the Chola [kingdom] had been on the offensive against Kerala for over hundred years. Kandan and Karuthamma had approached a priest known as Korman, praying for a solution to defeat the Cholas. It is said that they were told to fast for forty-one days so that they would have a son who could defeat the Cholas. So the 41-day fast emerges from Sree Ayyappan's birth. Sree Ayyappan, as the commander, mobilized the people against the Chola dynasty.

The temple of Sabarimala came into being after the *samadhi* (the final stage of life in which union with the dead is reached moments before or during death), of Ayyappa and the Mala Arayars continued to look after the temple until the 18th century. The temple has eighteen steps, that signify to the Mala Araya community—the eighteen hills that surround the shrine of Ayyappa. The community practised *'thenabhishekam'*—the bathing of the deity with honey. '*Then*' or honey, considered extremely precious in the wild and specifically in the lives of the tribal community. The Mala Arayars didn't enjoy this freedom for long, like the British conquest of India, the rituals and customs of the tribe was snatched away by the then ruling powers of the area. The Pandalam kingship incorporated their own beliefs into the sacred faith systems of the Mala Arayars, and attributed it to themselves. This becomes the point of origin for the alternate narrative associated with the claim of ownership of the temple in Sabarimala.

Thus, the lore of the Pandalam prince, Manikantan is brought up. The kingship strengthened their ties to the temple with the story of the Prince who was sent away into the forest only to return back with a tigress and her milk. The king therefore, upon the request of the prince set up an abode for him, some distance away from the palace. Later, the Mala Arayars were ousted from their living space surrounding Sabarimala—they were forced to flee deeper into the forests due to the actions of the kingship. Subsequently, The Pandalam rulers handed over the management of the temple to the Travancore Royal Devaswom Commission (TRDC), thereby creating a multifaceted, oblique history of the shrine, eventually misrepresenting it. An example would be about the eighteen steps which were seen as the eighteen mountains surrounding Sabarimala by the Mala Arayars, there was no religious connotation to it whatsoever. Moreover, the *neyyabhishekam*, (ghee showered) onto the deity is a relatively new practice. The Travancore Devaswom Board (TDB), after Independence, also intruded into the rituals and customs of the tribe. The *tantric* family, who are the Vedic head priests of the temple, still runs the temple under the aid of the Devaswom board.

Kerala has seen great social reformers like Sree Narayana Guru, Ayya Vaikundar and Chattampi Swamikal who have worked hard to make the temple proclamation come true. They were against the Brahminisation of the Hindu temples within Kerala. However, within the past decade, places of worship are increasingly being converted into places that propagate religious agenda. Accordingly, with respect to the aspect of caste disparity, progress has been painfully slow in Kerala, although there was a social reformation during the early twentieth century. It was only recently, in 2017 that a Dalit man was appointed as a priest in a temple for the first time. The shrine in Sabarimala and the deity exclusively belonged to the Mala Araya community. They were ousted from their lands and denied their right to indigenous practices, as is mostly the case of the other downtrodden castes within Kerala. The culture of the land is violated in order to satisfy a group of people who are economically, politically, physically and educationally powerful.

Firstly, with the encroachment of the traditional narrative, the Pandalam Rajas replaced the indigenous practises with their own lore associated with the sacred rituals. Secondly, with the transfer of control over the religious area to the TDB, and subsequent tantri interference in religious practice, the traditional customs underwent a second order transformation in the ascribing of previously unmentioned Brahminical rules of worship. It is in this respect that the gender disparity comes to focus.

It was in the 1950s that there was a fire at the temple premises and a renovation was undertaken to repair the damage. The temple was reopened the subsequent year and there was a rule brought forward which stated that, women between the ages of ten and fifty were barred entry from the place of worship. Even after the rule was brought forward, it wasn't very strictly enforced, women continued to enter the temple in the following years. In 1991, the traditional practice of feeding a newborn child (Rice Ceremony/*Chorunnu*), widely practised in Kerala, was held in the temple premises. The child's grandmother was the then woman executive officer of the Travancore Devaswom Board. It gained widespread popularity and many newspapers reported upon it. There were pictures to substantiate the claim. A writ was filed by different organizations at a later date enquiring about the entry of the women into the temple. In the same year, on April 5th, the Kerala High Court cross examined the claims of the then Sabarimala Tantri, upheld the earlier ruling of the Devaswom and asked to strictly enforce the gender-based restriction.

The restriction was imposed for women within the ages of ten and fifty, offering worship at the shrine. The High Court bench consisting of Justices K. Paripoornan and K.B. Marar respectively declared the prohibition imposed by the Devaswom board was not in the violation of the Articles 15, 25 and 26 of the constitution. It also did not violate the Hindu Places of Public Worship Act, 1968 (Authorization of Entry) as the prohibition was only in respect of women of a particular age group and not woman as belonging to a class or caste. It is to be noted that the prohibition on women's entry into the temples is 28 years old. The Supreme Court recently questioned the 1991 judgement of the High Court of Kerala and put forward a new judgement regarding the issue. The Supreme Court adjudged and reinstated the entry of women of all ages into the temple and its premises. Chief Justice Dipak Misra said: "Patriarchy in religion cannot be permitted to trump over the element of pure devotion borne out of faith and the freedom to practise and profess one's religion" (3). Meanwhile, Justice Chandrachud said, "To treat women as children of a lesser god is to blink at the Constitution itself. Among the fundamental duties of every citizen recognized by the Constitution is 'to renounce practices derogatory to the dignity of women.'" (23)

Here, the concept of 'double jeopardy' must be looked into. Double jeopardy is a term coined by Frances M. Beal to refer to the troubled life of black women in the 20th century. They had two issues haunting them. The first being their position as a woman and secondly them being African-Americans. The double conflict of race and gender is what creates this jeopardy. In Sabarimala's context relating to the tribe of Mala Arayars, the women were the most adversely affected. Firstly, they were women and secondly they were a part of a tribe not accepted then by the mainstream classes of society. The women there were given free will but it was taken away from them by the outsiders. They were violated by the upper class and were refused basic human rights. They are twice marginalized as put forward by Tapan Basu: Adivasis and Dalits are considered inferior by the majority, coupled with being a woman maximizes the issue.

The plight of the Mala Arayars has been ongoing. They are still not given their claimed birth right. The ban on women, and the loss of tribal rituals and culture within the context of the Sabarimala issue, reveals the very double jeopardy for the Mala Arayar women. Menstruation was considered a symbol of fertility, by the tribal people. Women and children went to the temple till the sixties. Archival records also show that young, upper-caste women from the Travancore region entered the temple till the eighties. Today, the Supreme Court has given the judgement regarding the entry of women into the shrine. It was one of their prerequisites. There were many protests by women against this, which shows the conservative view of a Brahminically conditioned section of the society in Kerala. This isn't anything new, when Sati was abolished in 1829 by the British, there were large scale protests by women across India practising it. But gradually it became an unnatural concept and practice. The Sabarimala issue might also cool down into a lesser impacted event in the coming years. The various political parties have pledged their allegiance to the issue but the community has decided not to involve themselves in any political horse-trade. The Mala Arayars are still fighting for their rights and Kerala knows about their struggles now.

The paper has accordingly examined the indigenous origins of the Sabarimala issue on two levels – that of encroachment of tribal cultural and ritual practices that has led to atrocities on the basis of caste and gender discriminations. Such an encroachment, we have demonstrated, has been propagated through

Brahmanism. Thus, the paper proves that Brahminisation is the true double jeopardy.

Works Cited

"Census India 2011—Population of India." *Census India 2011*, CensusIndia2011, n.d. http://www.censusindia2011.com.

Bambara, Toni Cade, ed. *The Black Woman: An Anthology*. New York: Pocket Books, 2005.

Basu, Tapan. "Narratives of Suffering: Dalit Perspectives." *Translating Caste*. New Delhi: Usha Offset, 2002. 181-96.

Gurukkal, Rajan. "Sabarimala through the Ages." *The Hindu*, 10 January 2019. https://www.thehindu.com/opinion/op-ed/sabarimala-through-the-ages/article25952897.ece

Iyer, Ananthakrishnan L. *The Travancore Tribes and Castes*. Trivandrum: Government Press, 1937. *Internet Archive*.

Konikkara, Aathira. "History Is Being Deliberately Neglected: Sabarimala and the Brahminisation of an Adivasi Deity." *The Caravan*, 28 October 2018. https://caravanmagazine.in/religion/pk-sajeev-sabarimala-mala-araya-brahminisation-adivasi-deity.

Mateer, Samuel. *The Land of Charity: A Descriptive Account of Travancore and Its People*. London: John Snow, 1871. *Internet Archive*.

Nair, Jaikrishnan. "The Photo That Took a Devout to Court." *The Times of India*, 29 September 2018. https://timesofindia.indiatimes.com/city/kochi/the-photo-that-took-a-devout-to-court/articleshow/66001604.cms

Photographer AP Joy Who Had Taken Photograph of the Controversial Photograph of 'Sabarimala Women in All Sorts.' *News 18 India*, 13 October 2018. https://malayalam.news18.com/news/kerala/photographer-a-p-joy-on-sabarimala-controversy-46745.html>.

The Supreme Court of India. *Indian Young Lawyers Association & Ors. versus The State of Kerala & Ors.* 28 September 2018. https://sci.gov.in//supremecourt/2006/18956/18956_2006_Judgement_28-Sep-2018.pdf.

Poems

Hues of pink and orange spread across the blues;
Like fire and ice melting into a poetic muse.
A scenery so soothing, yet so unjust to what a naked eye could do;
I wish I could pour life into you, for just a minute or two.
I would try to do justice deciphering you;
Because if passion and dreams had a common ground, it would definitely look like you.
One fine day, I woke up to a different sky;
The Monday morning blues gave me a different high.
Suddenly I saw her, brown, bold and beautiful;
She flew across the sky unarmed yet unshakable.
A bird like her, I was smitten the minute she crossed my way;
I'd be jealous if she chose anybody but me, so I began to pray.
She set her tiny feet on one of my branches, oh what a happy day!
Together we built a nest so beautiful, there's nowhere else I'd rather stay.
I promised her I'd never leave her side, ever;
While the other trees and birds would just fake it and sever.
Her family was happy with her choices, it was time that I made mine;
Some of my roots were growing old and unsupportive, some were doing fine.
My leaves were in pain, my branches falling apart;
She said she'd stay forever if I stood up for what I wanted, with all my heart.
She said "Talk to your roots, strengthen them, ask them to stand by you";

Stuck in my own thoughts, I didn't know what to do.
Today, as I look at the same sky while I breathe my last,
I know some other tree gave her the happiness that I couldn't;
While I died wishing that I fought harder for a forever with her in the past.

A. NIKITHA, USA

The Rainbow is Insane

The rainbow is insane
walking over Mahanadi
just as soon as the rain stopped.
I need time to think and find the thin sharp rays
streaming from the guts of the clouds. Wait,
what's the hurry? Let the birds dry their feathers
and the peacock his plume,
let the fish stick out their round mouths
for a draught of rainless air. But no!
She has to walk all over Mahanadi
and arch her back showing off her true colours.
The party is beyond the bank,
behind the big trees, if there are still some,
my memories had a vibgyor coloured dress once,
but, the butterflies stole them
and are gone; I don't seem to see them anymore.
It is the rainbow that came after the rain;
now here, now gone; insane
with all our colours; so much memory!
Sometimes it smudges over.

SHRUTI DAS, Odisha